MY PEOPLE PERISH

RELEASING THE POWER IN THE PEWS

DWIGHT MCGEE

"MY PEOPLE PERISH FOR LACK OF KNOWLEDGE" HOSEA 4:6.

My People Perish
by Dwight McGee
Copyright © 2022 Dwight McGee

All rights reserved. This book is protected under the copyright laws of the United States of America. This book may not be copied or reprinted for commercial gain or profit.

Scriptures marked KJV are taken from the King James Version Bible and rest in the public domain.

Scriptures marked NKJV are taken from the New King James Version®. Copyright © 1982 by Thomas Nelson. Used by permission. All rights reserved.

ISBN 978-1-63360-191-8

For Worldwide Distribution
Printed in the U.S.A.

Urban Press
P.O. Box 8881
Pittsburgh, PA 15221-0881

412.646.2780

Introduction	v
Chapter 1 **My Journey**	1
Chapter 2 **Background and Significance**	13
Chapter 3 **Knowledge of Vocal Spiritual Gifts**	18
Chapter 4 **Presence of New Testament Vocal Spiritual Gifts**	30
Chapter 5 **The Cessationist View**	47
Chapter 6 **The Seminar**	55
Final Thoughts	65
Appendix	70
Conclusion	95

INTRODUCTION

Almost all churches are united around biblical issues such as baptism, love, and obedience to the Ten Commandments. However, Christian groups tend to barricade themselves behind specific denominational beliefs and then tend to view anyone who believes differently as suspect at best or a heretic at worst. From my church experience, one of those beliefs is the existence and relevance of the spiritual gifts in today's church. On one hand, Pentecostal churches have always been identified by the belief in and expression of spiritual gifts like prophecy, miracles, and tongues.

On the other hand, groups like traditional Baptists seem to focus more on the life of Jesus Christ as presented in the gospels but not much on the principles and life of the early New Testament church. Because of this, Baptists maintain that spiritual gifts were instrumental in the days when the church was started but ceased to operate after the death of God's prophets and apostles.

Most traditional Baptist churches are more program and event-driven, whereas Pentecostals like services where they can "soak" in the presence of the Spirit. Baptist services are basically structured in a rigid form and strict adherence to it is paramount and believed to be "correct." If the Spirit of God chooses to visit, there is little time allowed for believers to embrace this experience with Him and one another. The order of the service must be followed and not the freedom of the Spirit—but Baptists would certainly claim they did follow the Spirit when they put the agenda together.

Yet the format is such that no one is expected to be heard from during the service other than the song leader, choir, announcement clerk, and the pastor at the time of the sermon—with someone perhaps praying on certain occasions. Of course, I am most familiar with Black Baptist churches, which have their own style that still adheres to the basic service structure I just described.

This has made the structure of their, or should I say our, services orderly and predictable. Messages are usually read from the pulpit with artistic flair that includes vocal inflections and hand gestures depending on the preacher's style, which in the Black Baptist tradition is usually quite animated with the expectation that the congregation will add a hearty "amen" or "hallelujah" from time to time. The conclusion of the message is announced in celebratory fashion which can include moans and melodious tones describing and summarizing the life of Christ as He went to Calvary, was nailed to the cross, hung there, died, was buried, but on the third day rose with power.

Sometimes this message of the journey to the cross and its aftermath seems to be pre-recorded and the written portion of the Word sounds vaguely like someone else's material. Pentecostal "Spirit-led" messages are experienced and delivered differently, which seems to me to be consistent with the fact that the written, inspired Word of God is designed to motivate and transform: "For the word of God is living and active and sharper than any two-edged sword, and piercing as far as the division of soul and spirit, of both joints and marrow, and able to judge the thoughts and intentions of the heart" (Hebrews 4:12).

In the Baptist setting, congregants are seen as members and the only ones seen as leaders or ministers are those who have leadership roles or titles. Individuals are not often taught that God has a ministry purpose for *all* in the body of Christ. Spiritual freedom is not as open as is seen in more Spirit-led churches. For a Baptist, order in the church is the hallmark of any service. Churches should have order, but the lack of training regarding spiritual gifts may be the bedrock of their dominant cessationist view (which is a word that means the gifts of the Spirit are no longer working in the Church today).

Baptists believe that a person receives everything he or she needs from God upon conversion with no subsequent post-conversion experiences with the Holy Spirit. God does the Spirit in-filling completely at the time of conversion. It is my premise in this book that increased knowledge and awareness of spiritual gifts are the means that will enable and empower traditional Baptists to walk in a life characterized by the fullness of the Spirit on an ongoing basis. In other words, if we teach the people what the word says about the gifts and ministry in the body (one individual to another), the Baptist church can regain some of what it has lost due to its adherence to its rigid order of service.

As their rule of interpretation, Baptists approach Paul's epistles and other books of the Bible literally. Thus contextual analysis and thinking are not regularly sought after or valued. By that, I mean we Baptists do not insert ourselves back into what the passage meant to the church that first read and received that word. Therefore, the Bible teaches us to "be filled with the Spirit" (Ephesians 5:18). What exactly did that mean to the Ephesians and how did it manifest itself in the life of the church and its meetings? Is that just a historical lesson for us of how the Spirit once worked or is it the standard by which He wants to work today in *all* churches?

When we assume we know what it means for us today, we can easily miss what more there could be because we think we already know. I maintain that contextual teaching and thinking could transform our minds to the point where we expect the Holy Spirit to do a work in the lives of believers after conversion and that includes the expression of His gifts through and in individuals—even in the public worship setting.

The Problem

I have been blessed to be part of churches in both Pentecostal and Baptist settings. As I write, I am the pastor of a Baptist congregation. Yet I earned my Doctor of Ministry degree from Oral Roberts University, an organization with Pentecostal roots, and was part of a Pentecostal church for many years. I draw regularly from both my Pentecostal and Baptist experiences and I am the better for it. I have seen the benefits and drawbacks in both settings, and I am mature enough to realize that no church or group of churches is perfect. We all see what we see (and sometimes only what we want to see) and believe it to be all there is, looking at anyone who sees something more or different as wrong and in error.

As I mentioned earlier, one area of contention is the role of the Spirit and the debate and acrimony around this issue are never in short supply.

Spiritual gifts have always been approached and taught with a number of misconceptions. Pentecostals see the gifts as "all or nothing." If you are in right standing with God, you have them and should be free to express them any time and in any place. The Baptists see them as "all is nothing." If you have them or want to express them publicly, you are in error.

Traditional Baptists in my ministry world have chosen to adhere to their "Doctrinal Resolution" as adopted in my region by the Oklahoma Baptist State Convention. This document addresses some of the spiritual gifts as described by Paul in 1 Corinthians 12. Five areas of particular concern are women in the church, the baptism of the Holy Spirit (the anointing), the utilization of tongues in the church, healing, and Bible prophecy. Let's look at what is stated about each one of these in the Resolution in the order I presented them.

Doctrinal Resolution

1. We believe as Baptists every believer is baptized into the body of Christ by God the Holy Spirit (1 Corinthians 12:13). This baptism takes place at the moment of salvation. The rite of water baptism symbolizes Spirit baptism. Spirit baptism is "the Anointing." (Ephesians 4:5; Matthew 3:11; Mark 1:8; Luke 3:16; John 1:33; Acts 1:5; 11:16; Romans 6:3)

2. Tongues in the church are mentioned in three books of the Bible, Mark 16:17; Acts 2, 10, and 19; and 1 Corinthians 12-14. We believe based on these passages of Scripture that tongues in the Bible in Acts 2 was a spoken dialect. Also, it was a written language and a spiritual gift used at the birth of the church and today has ceased.

3. We believe as Baptists that God is able to heal at will. However, we also believe as a Baptist

that no one individual has the "gift" of healing. The Apostles had special gifts of healing which the modern-day church does not possess. (Exodus 15:26; 1 Corinthians 12 and 13; James 5:16)

4. We believe as Baptists that no one can prophesy beyond what is written in the pages of Scripture. We further believe that Jesus Christ was God's final revelation to mankind. Therefore, we as Baptist believers do not believe in prophecy that cannot confirm the Scriptures. (see Hebrews 1:1-5; John 1:18)

There you have what Baptists believe in my district and it is much the same in every district. I cannot help but think that it is time to re-examine this stance to ensure that our preconceived notions of what we think these passages mean have not precluded what they could mean for the Church today.

My Purpose and Objectives

As I mentioned, I earned my Doctor of Ministry (DMin) at Oral Roberts University. The final part of any DMin degree is to present a ministry project, something that is academic in nature but also can be used and applied in a local church after it is completed. I chose to do something that focused on what I described earlier: the possible effects of increased openness to the Spirit in a Baptist setting. Therefore, the nature and purpose of this book is to present the findings of my DMin project that I submitted and was approved by my professors and evaluators at ORU.

I chose as my project the task of evaluating the existing knowledge regarding spiritual gifts among the members of Union Baptist Church. From there, I conducted some teaching and training on what the Bible had to say about spiritual gifts, after which I evaluated the impact and results. Let me be more specific about how I did this.

First, I administered a survey that included questions measuring the knowledge of those involved where spiritual gifts are concerned. Second, I embarked upon a ten-week teaching seminar (some of the material I will share with you later in the book so you can use it in your setting). Third, I gave the participants a post-seminar survey to measure the increase of their knowledge. This project was designed to expose them to new ways of thinking in order to cause a theological transformation and shift concerning certain doctrinal conclusions they held. In other words, once the congregants were exposed to more teaching about the gifts, would their attitude change and would they be more open to their expression in the church through those same congregants?

The pre-class survey questions were developed and administered to establish the foundation for the way forward and allow knowledge of, respect for, and consideration of all held views. In other words, I determined where people were at, so to speak, where the gifts of the Spirit were concerned. Were they lifelong Baptists or more like me with a diverse spiritual background? My goal then was to devise and present sound biblical and theological viewpoints regarding spiritual gifts in the ten-week training. The seminar was expected to increase the knowledge of the participants and was designed to be an open forum that promoted group interaction so everyone could hear from all the others. I didn't want it to be just me teaching and them listening. I wanted and needed an interactive platform from which the Spirit of God could open their eyes and minds.

Participants ranged in age from their eighties to their forties. This drastic diversity of age produced certain adjustment as the seminar unfolded to ensure everyone was learning at their own pace but making progress nonetheless. Older congregants needed individual attention to allow them to expand their understanding beyond the "this is how we've always done it" mentality. I was very sensitive while teaching the seminar because the project's ultimate goal was to broaden biblical understanding and empower congregants to be more deeply rooted and grounded biblically.

In other words, I was not teaching Baptist or Pentecostal doctrine, but rather looking at biblical stories and teaching about the Holy Spirit and its role in the Church from the Word of God with no preconceived agenda as to their meaning and application. Following the teaching seminar, the same survey questions were administered to measure the participants' increase of knowledge. I suspected that variables such as years following the Lord and how committed the participants were to the Baptist way of life would come into play—and they did. More on that later.

Why do I now present my findings to you in this book? I do so because I maintain that Unity Baptist is not much different from any other Baptist church—or to some extent to other evangelical churches. I believe our efforts at Unity Baptist to assess and increase the knowledge of our members concerning spiritual gifts caused them to be more open to the spiritual gifts and that will be good for the church and those who attend.

The project proved that once those gifts are presented biblically without any denominational labels, they can then be expressed in the life of the church, including public services, and also increase the confidence and engagement of the membership—which should be the goal of every local congregation. We should not only want to hold the attention of our Sunday "audience" so they can *hear* the truth, but also engage them so they can *apply* the truth in and outside the church walls.

Setting for the Project

My focus for my DMin project and this book remained constant and were best represented by two primary questions:

1. Would the teaching in a seminar of sound biblical foundations regarding spiritual gifts increase knowledge?

2. Would a person's age or educational status affect how he or she perceived biblical truth regarding spiritual gifts? Could they change? Would they?

Union Baptist Church, the congregation I pastor as I write, is located in Watonga, Oklahoma. It is a small rural church and is the result of a merger of the First Baptist

Church and Calvary Baptist Church in 1929. Other rural churches also disbanded around that time and people moved their membership to the Union Baptist Church roll. The congregation is diverse but predominately African American. Age varies throughout the Body, but there is a vibrant group of middle-aged congregants who are eager to be taught God's word. Other ethnic groups represent a small number but are also actively involved.

Before the COVID-19 pandemic, Sunday attendance averaged 50 to 75 people. Bible study convened on Wednesday night where attendance averaged between 30 to 40. (Please keep in mind that this was conducted and written prior to the pandemic, which has caused great upheaval and change throughout the world and in many churches. I will continue to present my conclusions, realizing that the impact of my work may look completely different once the pandemic is over and the "all clear" is given to meet in person.)

Union Baptist Church has been a pillar in the local African American community for decades. Services have been structured to be traditional and the polity is democratic. There has been one church split in its existence. Since its inception, this church has seen many pastors come and go. Union Baptist is affiliated with the National Baptist Inc. – USA.

Our twenty-first-century climate has created an eagerness in the church to modernize and seek the truth of God's written Word. Many members have taken a more active role of late and have raised questions regarding spiritual truths in the Bible, questioning prior teachings they have received and rigid doctrinal beliefs. Prior to becoming the pastor, I was known at Union Baptist Church having served as an associate on the ministerial staff. My appointment as pastor of this congregation in 2010 allowed me a broader ministry role due to my prior relationships with some of the members.

Forgive me if some of my academic background comes through in the pages you are about to read. As you would expect, my DMin project had to be a bit more than just the presentation of my project and findings. I had to back up my claims and work through a lot of research, some of which I will include for you to consider. I have distilled much of my DMin project work to the material you will read, and have taken out much that would not be of interest. If I have still included too much, just bear with me or move on the meat my work—which is the seminar, the results, and the way forward from here.

Pastor Dwight McGee, DMin
Watonga, Oklahoma
April 2022

CHAPTER ONE

MY JOURNEY

I have already alluded to my spiritual journey, but let me go back before we proceed and tell you a bit more about how I got to where I am today, the pastor of a Black Baptist Church in Oklahoma. I received my call to ministry in 1982. I began my journey where I was and assisted the churches I attended in the ministerial role as an associate to the pastor. While in that role, I became known as a somewhat rebellious regarding the traditional way of doing things.

I saw the hierarchy in the governmental structure of the local church perpetuated by the deacons and I questioned what they did and why they did it. It seemed to me to be a lifetime appointment to a certain role with a vague or non-existent job description. It also didn't seem that anyone was evaluated on the job they were doing as deacon (or any role for that matter). Later and with more maturity, I learned to operate with more humility and discernment, but at first, I questioned everything.

I didn't start my educational journey until 2003, more than 20 years later. The main reason I went back to school was my desire to engage in meaningful conversations and also answer questions related to the Bible and its doctrines with intelligence—handling the truth as befitting the things of God. I was also concerned that many people's approach to the Scriptures lacked any foundation in a historical background or context. In other words, they were stuck in narrow beliefs they did not get from the Bible but from what others told them was in the Bible—usually deeply influenced by their denominational beliefs. This just didn't seem right to me.

That is what prompted me to get more immersed in academic studies. Then I got involved in a college seminary and eventually began to pastor and teach. It was then that I was able to clearly see how relevant and important it is to be able to not only know the truth but also to be able to communicate it clearly—another concern I had.

It's sad that many people who have been in churches all their lives do not know the basic ABCs of biblical truth. That concerned me. It was interesting to see and to hear their personal perspectives of what Scripture meant to them and how they came to that conclusion because a certain person shared with them their own version of the gospel, which at times had no clear connection to biblical truth. That concern has been with me even now as I write this book. What do we believe? Why do we believe it? How do we communicate it? These are three important questions I hope to address in my ministry and this book.

One of the things that intrigued me in my Baptist experience has been the staunch opposition to spirituals gifts and the things of the Spirit in general. There are people in the pews of our churches who are wondering why that's so as well, which is one of the reasons I chose to proceed and do research proving my point that a person or congregation through the right teaching can acquire the truth and allow God to take them to another spiritual level where they participate and don't just spectate.

However, without understanding where their views and interpretations come from, people are stymied and plateau in their spiritual walk. I was able to acquire people with a wide range of church backgrounds and experience to form my target group for my project. I then taught about the gifts from a biblical and not denominational perspective, and it impacted their lives and the life of our church. You will hear much more on that later.

When I re-engaged with church life in the 1980s, I regularly heard that our youth are the future of the church. Having said that, there was never evidence of a time when we joined hands with the youth to lead them through the journey that would allow them to see, appreciate, and even question the different dynamics of local church life. When anyone would bring up questions, they (I could say we, for I was among them) were basically told, "We don't talk about or believe that. We're Baptists" and that was it. That was unacceptable to us. We were simply trying to discover on what they based their conclusions and practices and the answers we did receive were seldom adequate to satisfy us. I assumed if the Bible said it was so and we were a Bible-believing church, then we would and should follow what the Bible said. Since I was often the one raising the questions, sometimes on behalf of others, I was seen as the rebel.

    I was not content to stay where I was, so I determined to go a bit deeper and learn a bit more. I began my academic journey in 2003 by attending Redlands Community College. I took care of all my electives there in 18 months after taking a heavy course load. I transferred from there and went to Southwestern Christian University in Bethany, Oklahoma in 2006. I graduated with my bachelor's degree in 2008 and entered my master's program at Southwestern as well. I left there in 2009 to attend Oral Roberts University where I earned a Doctor of Ministry with an emphasis on Christian Biblical Leadership.

    I accepted my first pastoral position in 2010 and was then glad I had started my academic journey when I did. I went to school and completed that during that charge as well. The academic portion of schooling, especially in my undergrad and doctoral programs, was quite transformational and user friendly—if I can use that term. In other words, I was able to apply what I was learning directly to the church. It was user-friendly, not only to me, but for the people in the church. It gave us a bit of a cutting edge. Armed with research and new ideas, I was able to cultivate the soil in the church much differently than I could have previously. The people soaked up whatever I gave them.

    I have pastored two churches since 2010 and my second one has received the greatest benefit from what I have learned and they have grown spiritually. I've learned church growth is not always about the numbers, but about growing people spiritually. That's what's so exciting to me. I'm able to see the fruits of my labor because God has allowed us to grow spiritually because we have been true to what Paul wrote in Romans 12:1-2:

> I beseech you therefore, brethren, by the mercies of God, that you present your bodies a living sacrifice, holy, acceptable to God, *which is* your reasonable service. And do not be conformed to this world, but be transformed by the renewing of your mind, that you may prove what *is* that good and acceptable and perfect will of God.

We are being transformed as our minds are renewed through the study and proper application of what we are learning and it has made church enjoyable and challenging.

My current church is Union Baptist Church in Watonga, Oklahoma. During the COVID-19 pandemic, we followed the Oklahoma governor's guidelines as prescribed by the CDC and closed the church. At first, I did not feel confident or comfortable to hold online services, but eventually started "broadcasting" from my office. Then I expanded that to preach from my pulpit and put that out on Facebook Live while I kept in touch with the people in the church. Unfortunately, I lost a few of my Baptist colleagues to the pandemic and we are still feeling its effects in our district.

God used that, however, to help us grow as a church and help me grow as a leader. When we talk to the younger generation, we as older leaders must become more familiar with delivering ministry in non-traditional ways and that includes social media. I have to admit I am glad the technology piece was not part of my DMin studies for I had my hands full with the course material. Now let me get back to our discussion of how I used what I was learning from my university studies.

The assumption for my DMin project was that if we teach God's people from the Word, they will be more comfortable with the fact that they have spiritual gifts and will more readily offer them to help the church body grow. A key verse for me in my project is found in Hosea 4:6:

"My people are destroyed for lack of knowledge. Because you have rejected knowledge, I also will reject you from being priest for Me; because you have forgotten the law of your God, I also will forget your children."

I feel that if the teacher has the knowledge and God's people are taught the truth, then the people will be able to grow. That obviously means if the leader does not have the knowledge, then he or she has nothing to teach and the people consequently will not grow. Then they often rely on tradition and assume their tradition is the way it should be and biblically based. This means that it all depends on leaders and their desire and capability to learn new things and step out of their comfort zone. They must be stretched so they in turn can stretch the people so they can grow spiritually.

In essence, I'm saying that if we have a crisis in the church, it is a leadership crisis. If the people are willing and the Spirit is willing, the other component in the equation is leadership. Going where we have never gone will require courageous leaders who are willing to learn new things, not just fads, but strategies for growth prescribed by the Spirit.

Almost anyone who grew up in or is involved in the black church, no matter the denomination, is familiar with the artistic ability of the black preacher. When I came back to church as a young adult and since then, I have heard and seen a lot of good preaching. The problem I saw was that some if it was entertainment while some of it was secular. By that, I mean the preacher stopped short of expounding the word and instead focused on technique and delivery. I'm not against "celebration" in preaching but I always felt we should actually celebrate the revelation of the Word and not just use it as a means through which we get the congregation excited and "fired up." What's more, if we "celebrated" as part or at the end of each message, then hadn't that become a tradition rather than a means of enhancing the communication and understanding of what was preached?

I reacted to what I referred to as "filler" in the message—the theatrics, the whooping, and the artistic ability to impress to get the amens during the preaching—but the truth and content were not always there. There was no meat on the table. A lot of ministers and ministries emulated the more popular styles from high profile ministries, but I think our churches suffered for it.

Please don't misunderstand. I celebrate the preaching traditions of the Black church. At the same time, the technique must not become the message but must be used to serve the message. It's not about the preacher, but rather about the people who need a message from the Lord, in whose place we stand to speak on the Lord's day. If I was not careful, I too would be caught up in the presentation rather than the content, and I wanted it not to be either/or but both when I taught.

That is the reason I went back to school and kept going back to earn as many degrees as I could. And that's why I chose to teach the material you will see later not from the pulpit but as part of a seminar. That way, the focus would be on the content and not on the trappings and flow of a Sunday morning service. I wanted to prove that in order for us to be transformed as God's people, we must consider the methodology of our delivery. We've got to rethink that to make sure it is leading the people to know God's word rather than relying on the traditions of how the Word is delivered as opposed to what is delivered. We want to "have church" not when we have hooped and hollered but rather when we have hooped and hollered because we have heard from God through His word.

When God called me to Union Baptist and I accepted, I vowed that as pastor I would not to resort to the camp of traditionalism. I didn't believe God had brought me that far out of Egypt to have me turn around and go back to Egypt. I said we had to keep pressing forward and accept the stretching God had for us in the Promised Land. I saw firsthand how the people were stretched throughout our Bible studies, church services, and other times when we taught the word of God. I've seen positive and sometimes total transformation in God's people with the number I have. I know we're moving in the right direction, but I'm also cautious. I don't want to take the people too fast. And I want to make sure we don't go back to the old ways but instead keep pressing on to discover hidden treasures in new places.

That was one of the things that got me to finish my book now too. I decided to move ahead and try to work on them because that's something I've been putting on the back burner for so long. It's time for me to go ahead with these. God's given me some more ideas. I'm getting ready to begin writing more things, to try to get more publications done and spend more time busy rather than just relaxing.

If we have a leadership crisis in the black church (and we do), then I wonder if it is not because we are trying to fulfill our mission with half our team on the bench. By that, I mean that gifted women are forbidden, for the most part, from participating in public ministry roles. Women are totally excluded from standing behind the podium and declaring the gospel. However, they are allowed to stand down on the floor and give an address. Spiritual gifts that God may have chosen to give to women are the focus here and the above resolution has filtered down into many local bodies and has become an obstacle to spiritual growth, certainly for women but also for any believers who could benefit from the spiritual deposit the Spirit has given to all believers. Many have chosen to adhere to a doctrine or "official" document for the sake of remaining devout Baptists. During the pandemic, my district lost five pastors to the virus and we are struggling to find replacements. Part of the reason is that we cannot consider women for the roles. More on this later.

Part of the ambivalence about spiritual gifts is the issue of speaking in tongues which to some is essential for ministry and personal growth (Pentecostals) and for others it is anathema (Baptists). Some have experienced what they refer to as a visitation of the Holy Spirit and their testimony states that they do not understand what happened for they began to speak or babble in strange tongues and it was unstoppable. They have related that the experience began after a devoted prayer life when their praying in a known language transitioned to an unknown language.

There can be no question that the gift of tongues is

the most controversial and scrutinized of all the gifts. I will not engage an extended discussion on this matter for there is an abundance of material on the topic, both pro and con. I will say that the experience is biblical and the debate centers around whether or not the practice ended with the death of the last apostle.

One of the issues with speaking in tongues is the practice of interpretation. Is it for private devotions or can it be public in its expression? In some Pentecostal churches, an utterance in tongues can come from anyone in the congregation, after which people wait for someone, even the one who gave the utterance, for the interpretation. Traditional Baptists are more likely to believe the pastor is the only designated representative to give a word from the Lord as opposed to one coming from the audience.

Scripture states, "Let all things be done properly and in an orderly manner" (1 Corinthians 14:40) and this is usually the reason given for keeping a tight rein on congregational involvement in the service. They deem audience participation with the Holy Spirit not likely and Baptist pastors believe God will tell them first before He speaks to another.

Unfortunately, this philosophy has carried over into the expression of any or all gifts from the congregation. What if someone has a gift to pray for others to be healed? What if they have faith for miracles? From my experience, they will hold back, concluding it is not worth the embarrassment of being confronted by the pastor in the midst of the congregation—or even in private. Most individuals argue with themselves to know what the voice of God is and what it is not.

Traditional pastors choose not to consider the historical text when considering tongues and their interpretation—or the gifts in general. Where speaking in tongues is concerned, most have considered it worthless babbling that profits no one. They conclude it is easier to adhere to the doctrinal belief rather than spend the time in study or in instructing the people through trial and error—or more probably trial and success as God uses *all* His gifts to build up His church.

Through the decades, there has been an

over-spiritualizing of the texts that pertain to spiritual gifts. Sidney Greidanus shed light on this practice when he wrote, "'Spiritualizing' takes place when the preacher discards the earthly, physical, historical reality the text speaks about and crosses the gap with a spiritual analogy of that historical reality."[1] Failure to consider the historical-cultural situation of the text hinders contemporary readers from crossing that gap, so speak, to appreciate the relevance of the text(s) for today. When that happens, the passage or story becomes a relic and not a living, breathing principle. Most traditional pastors fail or refuse to accept that a text has relevance for that audience in this day and hour and can be prescriptive for modern day audiences. Morna Hooker remarks that "the gospel must be expressed in our own language and culture and situation if it is to be relevant."[2] It would make sense that we must use the techniques the Spirit chose no matter the era in which we live.

Some messages today from the traditional pulpit are filled with secularization that chooses not to challenge the lives of the audience. Most messages are taken from the four synoptic gospels. Old Testament passages are stories that have become so familiar in their use and interpretation as to be considered useless. Because of the narrowness and inflexibility of our rules for interpretation, we have often resorted to techniques of preaching and teaching rather than the illumination of the Spirit that can break out among the people when the Word is presented by anointed teachers—who have no need for rhetorical tricks to hold the people's attention or gain their approval through a hearty "amen."

When honest questions rise from one's personal study of the Word, one may meet opposition if certain biblical truths are brought forward for discussion and examination. The Bible challenges us to "be diligent to present yourself approved to God as a workman who does not need to be ashamed, handling accurately the word of truth" (2 Timothy

---

[1] Sidney Greidanus, *The Modern Preacher and the Ancient Text* (Grand Rapids, Mi: Williams B. Eerdsman, 1988), 160.

[2] Morna Hooker, "What Do We Preach about Jesus Christ?" *Epworth Review* 3/1 (1976):49-56; quoted in Sidney Greidanus, *The Modern Preacher and the Ancient Text* (Grand Rapids: Eerdmans, 1988), 158.

2:15). Problems tend to surface when individuals come into a truth and choose to challenge the traditional interpretation or practical expression.

Most traditional pastors are uncomfortable with and unprepared for these challenges. Leadership insecurities may arise due to the inadequate training a pastor has received, which makes them reliant on the interpretations passed on to them by others or by history itself. Some individuals have been told their role is not to question the pastor.

I find this most unfortunate in the areas of personal needs among the people. Healings are not pursued for members and most illnesses are prayed for outside the church service. When there is prayer, seldom is there faith for healing, only comfort. Pentecostals tend to confront the reality of illness right in their church services. The Bible is clear in asking the question, "Is anyone among you sick? Let him call for the elders of the church, and let them pray over him, anointing him with oil in the name of the Lord" (James 5:14).

A narrow interpretation of that will cause someone to call or email an elder for a private prayer session, but when would those to whom James wrote have accessed an elder? In all probability, it was during their public meetings. It was Jesus who told the disciples they had authority and power over all demons and to heal (see Luke 9:1) and that has not been revoked. There is *no* warning to do this only in private or small settings as opposed to the public meeting. Even Jesus healed in the public synagogue meetings, much to the chagrin of the leaders.

Media has served to portray the gifts in a negative manner. We have all seen the "church lady" or other comedians mock those who pray for the sick. This is because some TV evangelists come in the name of Christ to capitalize and prey on the poor for self-gain. Many wolves in sheep's clothing have been exposed through various scandals and unethical behavior, which has served to cast a shadow on those who have legitimate gifts of faith and healing—some of them not in full-time or official ministry positions.

Therefore, we have often made rules and issued official

statements with blanket procedures to deal with an expression of any gifts, even the legitimate ones. In order to avoid any problems, we have also banned any benefits. In other words, we have thrown out the baby with the bath water.

God can heal at His will and the mission of the church is simply to pray and that prayer can and must be both private and public. Public insecurities restrict the minds and actions of our members and these are reinforced from the pulpit. Despite the above Scriptures, many have been preached "at" for so long that it is dangerous for laypeople to express their gifts, which has been reinforced by scandalous evangelists.

With all due respect to those who hold a cessationist viewpoint (those who believe that the gifts ceased to operate upon the death of the last apostle), I quote from David Oss and his response to this view:

> The fact is that 1 Corinthians 12-14 is in the Bible. It tells us, along with Acts and the rest of the New Testament, what is characteristic and normal during the last days, not the apostolic era. This distinction between apostolic and sub-apostolic eras is foreign in the Bible and is only useful for describing the role of persons who founded the church (e.g., Eph. 2:20ff.), not for defining the nature of "the last days." To do the latter, one should search the New Testament with a view toward determining what is normal in the church during the period from Pentecost to the return of the Lord. There may be some differences in how the church applies the teaching of the New Testament, but there should be no difference in what the Bible teaches and what we believe.[3]

The Bible does not teach cessationism. It would be counterproductive to assume that God intended for gifts to be manifested in biblical times and not for modern day. Are we that sophisticated or beyond need today that we do not require the gifts? If the early church was encouraged to express

[3]David Oss, *Are Miraculous Gifts For Today: Four Views*, ed. Wayne A. Grudem (Grand Rapids: Zondervan, 1996), 171.

their gifts, is that simply for us to read as part of the history of the church or should be part of the life of every church?

We need the gifts to evangelize new believers and plant churches today as much as in the early church. The Word of God says that sign and wonders *are*, not *were*, to follow those who are in the Lord. Traditionalists and their allies have chosen to adhere to the cessationist view because there are few if any miraculous things going on in churches today. Many have chosen to evict or ban the Holy Spirit from the Church so they can adhere to a program or protocol, and maintain the status quo.

It is my conclusion that we must urgently invite the Holy Spirit back into the Church so miraculous signs and wonders may occur. God is still in the spiritual-gift-giving mode and we are the vessels He has chosen to use. Let me share more in the next chapter that will support the statement I just made.

CHAPTER 2

BACKGROUND AND SIGNIFICANCE

All evangelical believers serve God and believe His power is supernatural. They believe He *can* do anything He chooses but they are ambivalent about whether He *wants* to heal or give them other supernatural expressions today. Church historian Vinson Synan suggests that American Baptists had a tradition of the laying on of hands after water baptism. Synan further stated, "Though there seems to be evidence of charismatic activity among some early Baptists, in time the vast majority of the pastors and teachers in the churches adopted a 'cessation of the charismata' view of the gifts that was common in most churches."[4]

My doctoral project in which I introduced solid biblical proof that gifts should be present and operational in this modern era proved, as I will show later, that when we as leaders increase the knowledge and support the release of gifts, congregants were more confident to do so and the church benefited from it. Throughout the years, many Baptist leaders have been ostracized because of their Pentecostal experiences. Synan states, "Independent Baptist evangelists also made news in the 1950s in the heyday of the healing-deliverance

---

[4] Vinson Synan, *The Century of the Holy Spirit: 100 Years of Pentecostal and Charismatic Renewal, 1901-2001* (Nashville: Thomas Nelson, 2001), 185.

crusade movement. Among those claiming Baptist ordinations were William Branham and Tommy Hicks."[5]

Dr. Thomson K. Mathew stated that Jesus came and did three things: preach, teach, and heal. Dr. Mathew suggests that ministry in the 21st century has to be Spirit-filled, stating:

> Spirit-filled ministry is power-filled ministry. Jesus said, "All authority is given unto me." This authority was also given to His disciples, who were to continue the ministry of Jesus. Scripture states, "These signs will accompany those who believe." Signs, wonders, and miracles are possible today because the same Spirit that raised Jesus from the dead now dwells in us (Romans. 8:11). Jesus instructed us not only to preach and teach, but also to heal. Healing is a sign of the Kingdom of God and a gift of the Holy Spirit. Ministers have the privilege and the authority to pray for healing; whether their ministry is pastoral or evangelistic, a powerful ministry must include healing.[6]

Definitions

I defined spiritual gifts in my project as the *pneumatekos* gifts as described by Paul the Apostle (see 1 Corinthians 12:1). Walvoord and Zuck offer a sound theological definition for each gift:

> Wisdom refers to insight into doctrinal truth. Knowledge refers to the ability to apply doctrinal truth to life. Faith is an unusual measure of trust in God beyond that exercised by most Christians. Healing is the ability to restore health and also to hold off death itself temporarily. Miraculous powers will refer to exorcising demons or inducing physical disability or even death. Prophecy is the ability to declare a message of God for His people. To distinguish between spirits is the ability

---

[5] Synan, 186.
[6] Thomson K. Mathew, *Spirit-Led Ministry In The 21st Century* (New York: Xulon Press, 2004), 96.

to differentiate the Word of God proclaimed by a true prophet and a satanic deceiver. Tongues are the ability to speak an unlearned, living language. Interpretation is the ability to translate an unlearned language expressed in the assembly.[7]

Other words may be used throughout my project to illustrate a direct connection to God for spiritual intervention. "Pleading the blood of Jesus" is an old Pentecostal term that symbolizes the body or condition of the individual to be immersed into a supernatural covering that serves as a shield of protection. The "anointing" is another word that is often used to describe the Spirit of the living God flowing throughout one's body to overpower and remove certain physical conditions or diseases.

The Limitations

Most of those attending my gifts seminar were members of Union Baptist Church. I realized that some of the language and terms used in this project were unusual to some of the participants and may be to you as well. I also realize that your context may require a different approach or terminology when discussing the modern expression of spiritual gifts in churches. Many in my group were not traditional Baptists but all suffered from a lack of Bible training that resulted in many uncertainties as to what is true and untrue concerning gifts. Those involved in this study varied in age and socio-economic status significantly impacted their ability to increase their desire for more knowledge of spiritual gifts.

Some Assumptions

The first assumption was that those participating in this seminar had attained a basic level of Christian education. I determined that many involved in this study had heard about spiritual gifts but had chosen to avoid their practice either because of the lack of knowledge and/or a cessationist mindset. While each person's understanding differed regarding

---

[7]John F. Walvoord and Roy B. Zuck, *The Bible Knowledge Commentary*, An Exposition of the Scriptures by Dallas Seminary Faculty New Testament, (Colorado Springs, Colo: Chariot Victor, 1983), 533.

spiritual gifts, the interactive seminar engaged everyone at whatever level they had.

The next assumption was that there would not be an immediate response to participate in the seminar or express spiritual gifts because of lack of confidence and fear. Group interaction was encouraged to warm the climate of the seminar. Finally, the last assumption was that the Word of God would be the key to transform the intellect of those present toward spiritual gifts.

A Summary

Twenty-first century church is crying out for a sign from God to authenticate His reality. Churches cannot adhere solely to the traditions of men that have been pre-established but must rather become knowledgeable as to the entire Word of God to better equip themselves to emerge as leaders. Increased knowledge of spiritual gifts will enhance the sensitivity of the Holy Spirit that encourages and empowers the believer to stand boldly on the Word of God.

All believers need greater confidence to counteract the limitations that both lack of knowledge and historical interpretation have imposed. This impairment has crippled many and caused them to be satisfied to be pew members and not engage the world or others as bold men and women of God. Members in the church all agreed that they have heard powerful preaching with minimal content for much too long, thus not really being taught the written Word of God. This seminar and study were intended to facilitate knowledge and edify those present who then in turn can express their gifts and edify the body of Christ.

This project evaluated the pre-existing knowledge of the participants by asking questions related to the topic through two questionnaires, one before and one after. Examination of the results revealed a significant increase of knowledge and led to the conclusion that the information did indeed give people the release they needed from past assumptions to present involvement.

But before we get into the survey itself, let me spend a

bit more time looking at what the Bible has to say about what I have labeled vocal spiritual gifts—prophecy, tongues, and interpretation. Along with the biblical portions, I include a lot of research from my DMin project. This material was the material from which I drew the content for my workshop sessions in my church.

CHAPTER 3

KNOWLEDGE OF VOCAL SPIRITUAL GIFTS

The infallible Word of the holy Scriptures has always been the bedrock of both Pentecostal and charismatic doctrines. Accounts in the Word describe how the Spirit of God has shown Himself in His most powerful form to cause great changes throughout the Earth. For example, in the beginning, the Spirit of God moved over the surface of the waters (see Genesis 1:2). People of the ancient world often heard the voice of God, sometimes through his prophets, and through obedience to that voice, saw victories and blessings bestowed on them.

I explored the problems with and reactions to public manifestations of spiritual gifts in the previous chapter. In this chapter, let's examine more thoroughly the historical, biblical, and theological perspectives of what we call the gifts of the Spirit. I will provide a sound Pentecostal and charismatic underpinning for what I refer to as vocal spiritual gifts. We will look at a variety of biblical passages, works of theologians, and the thoughts of several Christian scholars. What is my purpose? It is to prove that the gifts have always been present in the Church and therefore the modern church must make room for them as well—regardless of tradition or preference.

Pentecostal and charismatic platforms have always drawn from the infallible Word of God to justify their theological stance regarding vocal spiritual gifts, whereas many African American Missionary Baptists oppose this theological stance and choose to believe that vocal spiritual gifts do not exist in this era of time. African American Missionary Baptists view the vocal spiritual gifts as being significant in the ancient world but have since ceased to operate, referred to as the cessationist interpretation.

It is my conviction that vocal spiritual gifts are in the plan of and necessary for God's kingdom work today; therefore, this chapter addresses the following questions: Are vocal spiritual gifts for today? Are Pentecostals standing alone in this area of understanding? Does the Bible provide evidence and instruction that vocal spiritual gifts are relevant for and active among believers today? (As we proceed, I have opted to keep some of the references that were in my original DMin project. My objective is to show that there are many who interpret ancient moves of the Spirit to be relevant for today's church and who also believe that those same Spirit moves are necessary for modern church growth and revival.)

Vocal Spiritual Gifts in the Old Testament

Vocal spiritual gifts are present in the Old Testament in the form of prophecy. Let's look at the lives or ministries of three prophets God used to bring forth His supernatural words and works. Moses, Ezekiel, and Joel are prophets of the Old Testament called of God to speak His divine Word. The book of Numbers in the Old Testament traces the plight of the Israelites through their wilderness experience as they are preparing to enter the Promised Land. Moses is seen in this Old Testament book as a leader chosen by God to direct His people through the word of prophecy. One author notes, "Moses was the Hebrew prophet who delivered the Israelites from Egyptian slavery and who was their leader and lawgiver during their years of wandering in the wilderness."[8]

---

[8] Ronald F. Youngblood, ed. "Moses," *Nelson's New Illustrated Bible Dictionary*, rev. ed. (Nashville, TN: Nelson, 1995), 859.

Numbers 11 records an account of when the nation of Israel complained about their living conditions. God had delivered His chosen people (Israel) from the harshness and bondage of Egypt. While on their way to the Promised Land, God provided them with manna from heaven for their daily sustenance. Eventually, they were dissatisfied with His provision and wanted a greater variety of food. Consistently, they cried out and complained to Moses that conditions had been better in Egypt: "We remember the fish which we used to eat free in Egypt, the cucumbers and the melons and the leeks and the onions and the garlic, but now our appetite is gone. There is nothing at all to look at except this manna" (Numbers 11:5-6).

Moses' response to their nagging complaints was to go to God as their designated servant and representative. The people's laments had become too much, and Moses found himself complaining to God. "So Moses said to the Lord, 'Why hast Thou been so hard on Thy servant? And why have I not found favor in Thy sight, that Thou hast laid the burden of all this people on me?'" (Numbers 11:11). Albert Butzer explains, "The burden of Moses' complaint was that he could not bear the heavy burden alone (the Hebrew word carry, bear, is the same as in vs. 12)."[9] Moses desired to die rather than view his wretchedness by not being able to meet their needs (vs. 15). Butzer further explains,

> The response of the Lord to the great distress of His prophet was twofold—mercy and curse: 1) there was mercy to Moses in that his work load was now to be shared by seventy leaders who will help him to carry the burden of the people in future encounters (vv. 16-17); 2) there was a curse on the people that was in kind with their complaint: they asked for meat and would now become sick with meat. (vv. 18-34).[10]

---

[9] Albert G. Butzer, "Numbers: Text, Exegesis, and Exposition." *The Interpreter's Bible*, vol. 2 (Nashville, TN: Abingdon, 1953), 196.

[10] Ronald B. Allen, *Genesis-Numbers*, The Expositor's Bible Commentary, vol. 2, ed. Frank E. Gaebelein (Grand Rapids, MI: Zondervan, 1990), 792.

Moses was instructed by God to choose seventy men from the officers of Israel to meet him at the tent of gathering to stand with him. When they obeyed this command, God would speak and share the Spirit of Moses with the other seventy. Thus, God provided relief in sharing the heavy load of caring for the people. Notice that God shared with the others the same Spirit Moses had. God promised to empower and equip the seventy with the same energy as Moses.

Israel's complaint had angered God because they neither appreciated nor acknowledged His ongoing provision for them. Therefore, God spoke the prophetic word to Moses: "And say to the people, 'Consecrate yourselves for tomorrow, and you shall eat meat; for you have wept in the ears of the Lord, saying, 'Oh that someone would give us meat to eat! For we were well off in Egypt.' Therefore the Lord will give you meat and you shall eat'" (Numbers 11:18).

The cry for meat caused God to act and He chose to supply Israel with a surfeit of meat. God explained to Moses that the principal issue was not meat but that His people had rejected Him as their Provider, murmuring that their omnipresent and omnipotent God treated them worse than their Egyptian overseers. God assured Moses that regardless of the number of people (estimates range from 600,000 to the millions), He would provide meat for them to eat for a month. The amount would be so much that Israel would eat it until it came out of their nostrils.

God reassured Moses that he would see His word come to pass. Perhaps Moses needed a refresher to be reminded of what God was capable of doing. Moses conveyed the message of God to the seventy who were gathered around the tent: "Then the Lord came down in the cloud and spoke to him; and He took of the Spirit who was upon him and placed Him upon the seventy elders. And it came about that when the Spirit, rested upon them, they prophesied" (Numbers 11:25).

One commentator wrote, "This verse contains terminology basic to an understanding of ecstatic prophecy. It is told of Saul that he came upon a band of prophets and was overcome by ecstasy. He could not resist its onslaught and began to prophesy ecstatically."[11] Moses clearly understood the Spirit of God and acknowledged that God was his source. The Spirit rested upon them, and immediately they began to prophesy. Clearly the Spirit of God was present for them to be able to prophesy.

"The outcome is that *when the Spirit settled down on them they prophesied*. It means, literally, 'to act the prophet.'"[12] The interesting part of this event is that two men selected by Moses, Eldad and Medad, chose not to follow him to the tent of the meeting.

> However, two men, whose names were Eldad and Medad, had remained in the camp. They were listed among the elders, but did not go out to the tent. Yet the Spirit also rested on them, and they prophesied in the camp. A young man ran and told Moses, "Eldad and Medad are prophesying in the camp." Joshua son of Nun, who had been Moses' aide since youth, spoke up and said, "Moses, my lord, stop them!" But Moses replied, "Are you jealous for my sake? I wish that all the Lord's people were prophets and that the Lord would put his Spirit on them!" Then Moses and the elders of Israel returned to the camp (Numbers 11:26-30).

It is interesting the same Spirit that rested upon the others at the tent rested upon those two as well. As the Spirit rested upon them, they were observed prophesying in the camp. God indicated that seventy men had to be selected and they were to consecrate themselves. It appears that sixty-eight went to the tent and two remained at the camp. God wanted His word to be evident both in the camp as well as the tent. Before we move on, let's look at how the story ended:

> Now a wind went out from the Lord and drove quail in from the sea. It scattered them up to two cubits deep all around the camp, as far as a day's

---

[11]Baruch A. Levine, *Numbers,* Anchor Bible, vol. 4A (New York: Doubleday, 1993), 325.

[12]Timothy R. Ashley, *The Book of Numbers*, New International Commentary on The Old Testament (Grand Rapids, MI: Eerdmans, 1993), 213.

> walk in any direction. All that day and night and all the next day the people went out and gathered quail. No one gathered less than ten homers. Then they spread them out all around the camp. But while the meat was still between their teeth and before it could be consumed, the anger of the Lord burned against the people, and he struck them with a severe plague. Therefore the place was named Kibroth Hattaavah, because there they buried the people who had craved other food (Numbers 11:31-34).

This punishment took many lives. Ashley summarizes, "The incident was memorialized by calling the place *Kibroth-hattaavah* (the graves of the craving)."[13]

Therefore, as we consider the hermeneutic or context for interpretation critical to any proper understanding of Scripture, we can see the historical relevance to the gift of prophecy. This was the way that God chose to communicate to His people. This word came in the form of instruction, warning, or exhortation. This experience reveals the importance of hearing and obeying the Word.

Ezekiel 37:1-14

The second Old Testament prophet to be considered is Ezekiel. Let's look at Ezekiel 37:1-14:

> The hand of the Lord was on me, and he brought me out by the Spirit of the Lord and set me in the middle of a valley; it was full of bones. He led me back and forth among them, and I saw a great many bones on the floor of the valley, bones that were very dry. He asked me, "Son of man, can these bones live?"
>
> I said, "Sovereign Lord, you alone know."
>
> Then he said to me, "Prophesy to these bones and say to them, 'Dry bones, hear the word of the Lord! This is what the Sovereign Lord says to these

---

[13]Ashley, 219.

bones: I will make breath enter you, and you will come to life. I will attach tendons to you and make flesh come upon you and cover you with skin; I will put breath in you, and you will come to life. Then you will know that I am the Lord.'"

So I prophesied as I was commanded. And as I was prophesying, there was a noise, a rattling sound, and the bones came together, bone to bone. I looked, and tendons and flesh appeared on them and skin covered them, but there was no breath in them.

Then he said to me, "Prophesy to the breath; prophesy, son of man, and say to it, 'This is what the Sovereign Lord says: Come, breath, from the four winds and breathe into these slain, that they may live.'" So I prophesied as he commanded me, and breath entered them; they came to life and stood up on their feet—a vast army.

Then he said to me: "Son of man, these bones are the people of Israel. They say, 'Our bones are dried up and our hope is gone; we are cut off.' Therefore prophesy and say to them: 'This is what the Sovereign Lord says: My people, I am going to open your graves and bring you up from them; I will bring you back to the land of Israel. Then you, my people, will know that I am the Lord, when I open your graves and bring you up from them. I will put my Spirit in you and you will live, and I will settle you in your own land. Then you will know that I the Lord have spoken, and I have done it, declares the Lord.'"

We read that "Ezekiel was a prophet of a priestly family carried captive to Babylon in 597 B.C. Ezekiel prophesied to the captives who dwelt by the River Chebar at Tel Abib."[14] Ezekiel 37 reveals the prophetic work of God. In that chapter, God used His prophet Ezekiel to speak a word to a useless

---

[14]Youngblood, "Moses," 429.

nation to revitalize them with hope from His spoken word. "Chapter 37 begins without any transition, simply revealing the apocalyptic vision that concluded Ezekiel's message on Israel's future restoration. This vision pictures the manner in which the Lord would restore His people. Some believe this event did not really take place but rather was a vision given to Ezekiel to symbolize Israel's future restoration."[15]

The vision or event took place in the valley of the Euphrates River in Babylon, probably the same valley that was mentioned in chapter three. The valley was full of dried, sun-parched, good-for-nothing bones. One commentary remarked, "'The hand of Yahweh was upon me,' indicating the state of trance in which the vision was experienced."[16] The Bible suggests Ezekiel was in the Spirit when he was led into the valley. God addressed Ezekiel with a question and asked, "Can these bones live?"

Ezekiel was wise in that he chose not to answer God because he knew the power of God extended even into the realm of death. Hall explains, "The prophet answered the challenge to faith by saying that his faith was small, but that the God of his faith was great."[17] God commanded Ezekiel to prophesy over the bones. The prophecy was plain and simple: "O dry bones, hear the word of the Lord" (verse 4). Prophecy is bringing the Word of God and applying it to the problems of people. According to Hall, "Prophecy is not only a foretelling but rather a forth telling."[18] Ezekiel brought forth the Word of God to the dried bones to resurrect them from their graves of hopelessness, a similar situation in which some churches find themselves today.

Ezekiel recorded the word of the Lord: "Behold, I will cause breath to enter you that you may come to life. And I will put sinews on you, make flesh grow back on you, cover

---

[15]Ralph H. Alexander, *Ezekiel*, The Expositor's Bible Commentary, vol. 6, ed. Frank Gaebelein (Grands Rapids, MI: Zondervan, 1990), 924.

[16]Joseph Blenkinsopp, *Ezekiel,* Interpretation Bible Commentary, ed. James Luther Mays (Louisville, KY: John Knox, 1990), 170.

[17]Bert H. Hall, *Jeremiah, Lamentations, Ezekiel, and Daniel*, The Wesleyan Bible Commentary, vol. 3 (Peabody, MA: Hendrickson, 1979), 467.

[18]Hall, 467.

you with skin, and put breath in you that you may come alive; and you will know that I am the Lord" (verses 5-6). The Bible bears witness that Ezekiel obeyed God and immediately there was a rattling noise. Hall notes, "The Hebrew may be translated literally, and there was a voice, as I prophesied, and, lo, a rustling, and the bones come together."[19] As Ezekiel prophesied, the voice of God was heard and made the bones tremble and shake.

The Bible illustrates two stages of life in that passage. Ezekiel prophesied the first time, and God clothed the bones with sinews, muscles, and tendons. The second prophecy gave breath, or the Spirit of God, to the lifeless bodies to reestablish life. The infallible Word of God was clear that when the Spirit of God entered the lifeless bodies, they all stood to their feet as a great army. Blenkinsopp asserts, "It is the Spirit activated prophetic preaching which bonds the community together and gives it the will to live and accept its future."[20] Ezekiel's obedience to God revealed that humankind is resurrected from the state of being hopeless through the injection of prophecy. Life is sustained through the Word *and* Spirit of God.

I feel that churches are prone to over-spiritualize the word of God or perhaps lean to a personal interpretational knee-jerk reaction rather than spending time with God and hearing for themselves. If these servants of God spent time with God and spoke the word of God, they would see that these biblical illustrations contain and serve to clarity the very essence of God. These are life-and-death matters for obedience results in life and disobedience in death, at least of a spiritual nature.

Joel 2:1-28

The last Old Testament prophet I will consider is Joel. The book of Joel detailed the plague of locusts that devastated the land and depleted all agricultural resources: "What the gnawing locust has left, the swarming locust has eaten; And what the swarming locust has left, the creeping locust has eaten; And what the creeping locust has left, the stripping

---
[19]Hall, 467.
[20]Blenkinsopp, 173.

locust has eaten" (Joel 1:4). According to one author, "To the prophet, the 'day of the Lord' was near (1:15; 2:1)."[21] He further noted that the "day of the Lord" is a time in which God will intervene in history.[22] Joel referred to this event twice in chapters one and two and the Babylonian army did indeed destroy Jerusalem in 586 BC.

God spoke to the prophet Joel to issue a call for the people to return to Him. God commanded Joel to tell the people to "consecrate a fast" (Joel 1:14). If the people chose not to return to God, they would have to suffer the terrible day of the Lord. The people were obviously familiar with the traditional practices of fasting: "How should a people return to the Lord?" Joel 2:12-13 frames the traditional practices of fasting with the assertion that a true return to the Lord is a matter of the heart."[23] Joel was clear in communicating to the people why they should return to the Lord and reassured them in Joel 2:13 that God is gracious, compassionate, slow to anger, and abounding in love.

God refreshed the call to Joel in 2:15 to "blow the trumpet and consecrate a fast." God instructed Joel to gather the people. "Spare thy people, O Lord" (Joel 2:17) was the cry God gave that Joel was to communicate to the people of God. Obedience to this prophetic message would cause the all-loving, most gracious, and slow-to-anger God to initiate deliverance. All that had been devastated and condemned would be restored and forgiven.

Joel continued his prophetic message by letting the people know, "You shall have plenty to eat and be satisfied. And praise the name of the Lord your God, who has dealt wondrously with you; then my people will never be put to shame" (2:26). In verse twenty-seven, God was clear that through these signs and wonders of replenishment, He is the God of His Word and beside Him there is no other.

Faith in Israel's God brings deliverance from judgment. Joel pointed out in 2:28-32 that the intent of the Lord was and

---

[21] James Linburg, *Hosea-Micah*, Interpretation Commentary (Atlanta, GA: John Knox, 1988), 63.

[22] Linburg, 63.

[23] Linburg, 66.

still is to pour out His Spirit on all flesh, a promise that was revisited on the day of Pentecost as Peter tied this promise to what the onlookers beheld when they all spoke in other tongues (more on this below). This was not to be an impartation only to select individuals but to all—male and female, old and young.

John Thompson suggests, "All flesh could mean all mankind, as in Isaiah 40:5, but the following possessives, your sons and daughters, show that the phrase here means all Israel. Previously the spirit of prophecy had been limited to a chosen few, but under this new dispensation God's revelation will come to both male and female, to both old and young, and even to the servant class."[24] A renewed spiritual encounter would encompass prophesying, dreams, and visions.

According to the prophetic message of Joel, the hearts of humankind had to return to the Lord before the Lord would choose to pour out His Spirit. It was to be after the people returned to God that He would prepare the people for an impartation from the Holy Spirit. John Thompson also asserts that the gift of prophecy enabled the prophets and those in the future to have the ability to discern and declare the will of God.[25] It was in and through Ezekiel's vision that the Spirit of God gave life to the dried bones. Lindburg concludes, "To receive the Spirit is to receive power, which can manifest itself both in acts (mighty deeds) and words (prophecy)."[26] Prophecy, dreams, and visions are all biblical means of the revelation of God.

In conclusion, the Book of Joel clearly defines the results of turning away from God.[27] Failure to acknowledge the grace and love of God can result in devastating conditions. However, Joel in the Spirit was found proclaiming a word from God that caused His people to consecrate themselves and return to Him with their whole heart. Returning to God

---

[24] John Thompson, "Lamentations-Ezekiel-Daniel and Twelve Prophets," *The Interpreter's Bible,* vol 6, George A Buttrick, ed. (Nashville, TN: Abingdon, 1956), 752.
[25] Thompson, 752.
[26] Linburg, 71.
[27] Linburg, 64-65.

and becoming faithful can cause God to reverse the curse on mankind and replenish all that had been wasted. It can also be the answer for a modern church in decay and decline.

We have examined some of what the Old Testament has to say about the vocal gifts. Now let's move on and take a look at the more important aspects of my case for the vocal gifts having an important place in the church, which I draw from the New Testament.

CHAPTER 4

PRESENCE OF NEW TESTAMENT VOCAL SPIRITUAL GIFTS

As we did with the Old Testament, let's take a quick look at some New Testament examples of and explanations for vocal spiritual gifts: tongues, interpretation of tongues, and prophecy.

1. Acts 2:1-21

It has been noted in the Old Testament that the prophet Joel spoke a prophecy indicating there was to be "a pouring out" of the Spirit of God, and Luke gave evidence in Acts 1:8 that the Spirit would empower the disciples as witnesses by "coming upon them." There seems to be a correlation or kinship with the language used both in the Old and New Testaments.

Luke clearly indicated that the day of Pentecost is the

day God chose to pour out His Spirit. "And when the day of Pentecost had come, they were all together in one place. And suddenly there came from heaven a noise like a violent, rushing wind, and it filled the whole house where they were sitting" (Acts 2:1-2). John Stott suggests the day of Pentecost was the final act of the saving ministry of Jesus before the Parousia.[28]

Stott further suggests Pentecost was the fulfillment of the promise and was the first revival of the church to visualize the unusual visitation of God.[29] One of my professors, Dr. Trevor Grizzle in his class on *The Book of Acts*, brought out the fact that Pentecost was a strategic time God chose to unite all people and universalize the gospel of Jesus Christ to all nations.[30] Gentiles as well as Jews were privileged to experience the outpouring of the Spirit to be inclusive for His work of the ministry.

Stott explains, "We do not know, therefore, if the 'house' of verse two is still the upper room or one of the many rooms or halls of the temple.[31] Luke seems to have a greater concern on the *when* and not the *where*. Some believe it was in a house, and others believe that it may have been a room in the temple. Luke stated they were all together in *one place*. Though it remains unclear on the actual geographical setting, the fulfillment of the promise is still biblically sound.

Luke points out that John the Baptist in his message stated, "As for me, I baptize you with water; but He who is mightier than I is coming, and I am not fit to untie the thong of His sandals; He Himself will baptize you in the Holy Spirit and fire" (Luke 3:16). Luke connected John's prophecy of the baptism "with the Holy Spirit and fire" with the miracle of Pentecost (Acts 1:5; 11:16). Luke described the coming of the Spirit in three distinct signs: a sound, a sight, and strange speech. Longnecker explains, "In vv. 2-4, three signs of the

---

[28] John R. W. Stott, *The Message of Acts* (Downers Grove, IL: InterVarsity, 1990), 60.

[29] Stott, 61.

[30] Trevor Grizzle, "Book of Acts," class notes from GBID 626, Oral Roberts University, September, 2009.

[31] Stott, 61.

Spirit's coming are reported to have appeared, each of them, wind, fire, and inspired speech, being considered in Jewish tradition as a sign of God's presence."[32]

The Lukan account describes the wind filling the house. These eruptions of the sounds of heaven were once again found restoring life. This is believed to be the same wind that Ezekiel prophesied about and called forth when life was restored to the dried bones, and it was this wind of God's Spirit that was to usher in the Messianic Age. Luke identifies this sign of the Spirit's coming to the believers of Jesus Christ as 'a noise like a violent, rushing wind'" (Acts 2:2).

This sign became visible to all in the form of "tongues of fire" (Acts 2:3). According to Willimon, "Fire was as a symbol of the divine presence among the first-century Jews."[33] John the Baptist linked this sign with his message that the coming Messiah would baptize with fire (see Luke 3:16). Luke further suggested that these tongues of fire rested on each one of them (Acts 2:3). Willimon further stated, "With playful ambiguity Luke expands these fiery tongues into the gift of 'other tongues' that the Spirit miraculously enables the assembly to speak."[34]

Diverse reactions were observed as the scene shifted from the Upper Room to the community. The diverse community gathered for the festival from all over the ancient world was bewildered because of the vocal expressions from those who received the Holy Spirit. Luke recorded "that they were all filled with the Holy Spirit and began to speak with other tongues, as the Spirit was giving them utterance" (Acts 2:4).

Luke gave assurance that it was the presence of the Holy Spirit that enabled the believers to speak in languages with which all were familiar. The Holy Spirit language was not unintelligible but was comprehended by the Jewish crowd: "And how is it that we each hear them in our own language to which we were born?" (Acts 2:8). John Polhill raised the question,

---

[32]Richard N. Longenecker, *John-Acts*, The Expositor's Bible Commentary, vol. 9, ed. Frank Gaebelein (Grand Rapids, MI: Regency, 1990), 270.

[33]Gaebelein, *John-Acts*, 270.

[34]William H. Willimon, *Acts, Interpretation: A Bible Commentary for Teaching and Preaching* (Atlanta, GA: John Knox, 1988), 30.

What is one to make of their speaking in "other tongues"? Does this refer to their speaking in language other than their own native tongue, or does it refer to the phenomenon of glossolalia, speaking in tongues, the ecstatic "Spirit language" Paul dealt with in 1 Corinthians 12-14? Or does it refer to a miracle of hearing as well? A good case can be made for each of these views. Those who consider the miracle to be speaking in tongues can point to its being a well-attested, early Christian phenomenon (1 Corinthians 12-14) as well as to its seeming appearance elsewhere in Acts 10:46; 19:6. It is described as "declaring the wonders of God" in verse 11, and this could be likened to Paul's description of tongue-speaking as speaking to God and speaking mysteries in the Spirit (1 Corinthians 14:2).[35]

Polhill further suggests that the word "tongues" in verse four may draw opposition, but in verse eight "language" is clearly to be interpreted as known language. The perplexity of the Jewish crowd shifted to mockery attributing this phenomenon to drunkenness (see Acts 2:13). Galileans were excluded from God's blessings in the sight of the Diaspora Jews and did not have the relationship or the ability to speak a dialect native tongue from countries far from Galilee in northern Judea.

William Willimon insightfully explains, "This miracle here is one of proclamation. Those who had no 'tongue' to speak of the 'mighty works of God' now preach."[36] Stott explains, "Those of us, who have confidence in Luke as a reliable historian, however, let alone as an inspired contributor to the New Testament, conclude that it is not he who is mistaken, but rather his rationalistic interpreters."[37]

Luke then presented Peter as being the representative of and spokesman for the Twelve to be the spokesman

---

[35] John B. Polhill, *Acts*, New American Commentary (Nashville, TN: Broadman, 1992), 98-99.
[36] Willimon, 32.
[37] Stott, 66.

to clarify this Spirit-filled phenomenon that occurred on Pentecost. Luke implies that it was the "filling with the Holy Spirit" that empowered Peter with the boldness to speak to the crowd. Polhill notes, "Whatever the actual phenomenon at Pentecost, Peter emphasized here that it was prophecy, inspired utterance from the Lord."[38] Peter reiterates the passage of Joel to validate the sights and sounds of Pentecost:

> And it shall be in the last days, God says, that I will pour forth of my Spirit upon all mankind; and your sons and your daughters shall prophesy, and your young men shall see visions, and your old men shall dream dreams; Even upon My bondslaves, both men and women, I will in those days pour forth of My Spirit and they shall prophesy (Acts 2:17-18).

2. A Comparison of Joel 2:28 and Acts 2

Linburg asserts, "Joel 2:28-32 has been given a unique honor in the history of the Christian church because it was the text for the first apostolic sermon, preached at Pentecost by Peter (Acts 2)."[39] Luke precedes the fulfillment of Joel's promise in Acts 2 by identifying in Acts 1 the purpose of the outpouring of the Spirit. Luke exchanged the language of Joel to say the promise is "coming upon," whereas Joel had said it would be a "coming upon." Joel began his prophecy with "it will come after this," and Luke again converted the language to say, "in the last days." Both of these phrases assure us that the Spirit is to come upon and infill the body of believers so they can become effective witnesses until the Day of the Lord's return.

The Holy Spirit is the only person who has been identified who will come upon and tabernacle in the bodies of God's people to continue the work and ministry of Jesus Christ: "But ye shall receive power, after that the Holy Ghost is come upon you: and ye shall be witnesses unto me both in Jerusalem, and in all Judaea, and in Samaria, and unto the uttermost part of the earth" (Acts 1:8).

---

[38] Polhill, 109.
[39] Linburg, 71.

The Old Testament illustrates God pouring out His Spirit upon certain people to perform a certain task, whereas the New Testament places the Spirit as an infilling experience for all believers who call on the name of the Lord. Acts 2 clearly suggests that they were *all* filled with the Holy Spirit. Linburg suggests people receive power upon receiving the Spirit. The Spirit was the enabler who equipped the apostles to be effective witnesses until the Day of the His return:

> And with great power the apostles gave their testimony (Acts 4:33), as well as through acts; after healing the lame man, the apostles say that the power to heal came from God (Acts 3:12). The ministry of Jesus is described in terms of the Holy Spirit and power, which enabled Jesus to do good works and to heal (Acts 10:38). Stephen is described as doing great wonders and signs, 'full of grace and power. (Acts 6:8)[40]

Peter's message validates the above in Acts 2:17-21:

> "And it shall come to pass in the last days, saith God, I will pour out of my Spirit upon all flesh: and your sons and your daughters shall prophesy, and your young men shall see visions, and your old men shall dream dreams: And on my servants and on my handmaidens I will pour out in those days of my Spirit; and they shall prophesy: And I will shew wonders in heaven above, and signs in the earth beneath; blood, and fire, and vapor of smoke: The sun shall be turned into darkness, and the moon into blood, before the great and notable day of the Lord come: And it shall come to pass, that whosoever shall call on the name of the Lord shall be saved."

Therefore, the comments of Joel and Peter are found to intertwine and support one another. The prophetic promise that the Spirit would come by Joel was found to be fulfilled on the day of Pentecost.

---

[40]Linburg, 72.

Exegesis of 1 Corinthians 12:1-11:
The Historical Context

Let's exegete 1 Corinthians 12:1-11 to continue our study of the gifts in the New Testament church in an attempt to uncover or discover their role in the modern church. Paul first preached the Gospel at Corinth during his second missionary journey. Paul made his living through his trade as a tentmaker or leather worker. Paul always began his ministry in any location by attempting to convince all who attended the synagogue of Jesus' Messianic legitimacy. He told Jews and Gentiles that Jesus Christ was God's anointed and soon-coming King.

Paul's ministry at Corinth was enhanced upon the arrival of Timothy and Silas because they brought gifts from the Macedonian churches that gave Paul more time to minister since he did not have to work. As Paul's ministry increased, so did opposition to it. Paul's ministry moved to the house of Titus Justus, and it was through his evangelism that many pagans came to know the Lord Jesus Christ.

D. A. Carson, Douglas J. Moo, and Leon Morris acknowledged, "Paul approached Corinth 'in weakness and fear, and with much trembling' (1 Corinthians 2:33) but was encouraged by a dream in which the exalted Christ assured him of safety and much fruit "(see Acts 18:9-10).[41] Ronald Youngblood agrees that after a short stay in Athens, Paul came to Corinth "in weakness, in fear, and much trembling" (1 Corinthians 2:3).[42] Youngblood points out that Corinth was viewed as a wicked city and seemed less likely to accept the message of the Gospel; however, Paul's stay lasted for eighteen months and many converts were made.

Apollos and Peter came to build on the foundation of Paul; however, partisan groups developed as a result of spiritual immaturity in the Corinthian community as they chose

---

[41] D. A. Carson, Douglas J. Moo, and Leon Morris, *An Introduction to the New Testament* (Grand Rapids, MI: Zondervan, 1992), 264.

[42] Ronald F. Youngblood, ed., "apostle Paul," *Nelson's New Illustrated Bible Dictionary*, rev. ed. (Nashville, TN: Nelson, 1995), 953.

to identify and follow various leaders. The church as a whole was not happy with Paul's leadership, and many problems emerged. Carson, Moo, and Morris described these problems as follows:

> The integrity of its life was marred by the abuses at the Lord's Table (11:17-34), at least one case of immorality (5:1-5), public litigation among members (6:1-8), uncertainties about the place of marriages (chapter 7), the propriety of eating foods sacrificed to idols (chap. 8), infatuation with the more spectacular of the charismatic gifts without any profound commitment to mutual love (chapters 1214), and a decidedly aberrant view of the resurrection (chapter 15).[43]

Youngblood agreed when he described the church of Corinth as a large and lively church that was deficient in moral and spiritual integrity. This insufficiency caused Paul much concern and was the cause and focus of the letters he wrote to the Corinthian church. Paul received much of his information from the household of Chloe and her reports revealed the hideous factionalism in Corinth. Robert Gundry agreed that the Corinthian church had "aberrant beliefs and practices of astonishing variety and vulgarism flourished."[44]

Gundry added that Paul was prompted to write his letter because of the report of the household of Chloe and because of the three delegates from the church, Stephanas, Fortunatus, and Achaicus.[45] Gundry further noted that Paul had written many letters earlier that have been lost and not preserved, but we know that the church of Corinth had written Paul asking for advice regarding marriage and foods sacrificed to idols.[46] Gundry also suggested that the Corinthian church had problems that warranted Paul to write this letter

---

[43]Carson, Moo, and Morris, 264.
[44]Robert H. Gundry, *A Survey of The New Testament* (Grand Rapids, MI: Zondervan, 1994), 359.
[45]Gundry, 360.
[46]Gundry, 360.

in an attempt to solve the issues that were causing such rampant division in the body of the church.[47]

Authorship and Date

In the beginning of this epistle, Paul clearly identified himself as the author, identifying himself as an apostle of Jesus Christ. Youngblood identifies Paul as the author of both First and Second Corinthians and further suggests, "that this epistle was written in Ephesus during Paul's third missionary journey perhaps in A.D. 56."[48] The first epistle is really believed to be the second letter written by Paul because the first is believed to have been lost.[49] Clarence T. Craig suggests that Paul stayed longer in Ephesus, and through this wide window of time, had the chance to write 1 Corinthians in AD 54.[50] Craig further believed that it is unnecessary to discuss the authenticity of the letter, because it has only been denied by fanciful scholars who have looked upon the Pauline correspondence as falsifications from the second century.[51]

Context and Analysis

Paul addressed a series of issues that have been brought to him by the Corinthian messenger party, including issues regarding marriage, divorce, celibacy, idolatry, diet, Christian freedom, worship, and spiritual gifts. Speaking to all the irregularities in the church, Paul then turned his attention to the issue of spiritual gifts and their exercise in the public assembly. Paul wanted the Corinthian church to know God had to be glorified for the benefit of others in their public gatherings, which were not to become occasions for the use of gifts for personal gain or self-satisfaction.

Most of these questions were stirred up by a group called the Judaizers, whose motive was to discredit Paul and destroy his works by insisting that Gentile believers had to

---

[47]Gundry, 360.
[48]Youngblood, "apostle Paul," 300.
[49]Gundry, 360.
[50]Clarence T. Craig, "Corinthians, Galatians, and Ephesians," *The Interpreter's Bible*, vol.10, George A. Buttrick, ed. (Nashville, TN: Abingdon, 1953), 13.
[51]Craig, 13.

follow the Law of Moses after salvation. Many Corinthian converts had previously been influenced by paganism and idol gods, and this also seemed to cause ongoing problems. Paul therefore suggested a simple test to reveal the real converts and prophets: "Therefore I make known to you, that no one speaking by the Spirit of God says, 'Jesus is accursed;' and no one can say, 'Jesus is Lord,' except by the Holy Spirit" (1 Corinthians 12:3).

These prophets believed their visions, revelations, and messages were from Christ, but they denied the humanity of Christ. Paul was clear in his counsel that only believers speaking by the Holy Spirit could and would acknowledge that Jesus Christ is Lord. They would affirm Jesus in humanity and also Jesus in His deity. Paul referred to God, Jesus, and the Holy Spirit in 1 Corinthians 12:3, but then he chose to stress the significance of unity of the Godhead in relationship to the gifts.

In verses four through six, Paul was clear in his language that there are diversities of gifts, differences of administrations, and diversities of operations, but it is the same God who works in all. The source of the gifts was the Spirit of God, and they were to be used for the common good of the body of Christ and not personal enrichment. W. Eugene March addressed this issue and stated that Paul's thoughtful reflections on this matter reveal at least three key matters:

First, in the midst of his personal anguish over the Jews' failure to recognize

> God's saving deed in Jesus Christ, Paul nonetheless believed the Jews—though disobedient—still to be God's people (Romans 9:2-5; 10:18-21; 11:2-6, 25-32), the "rich root of the olive tree" (11:17-18). Second, Paul's audience consisted of Gentile Christians, not Jews, who were concerned over whether they were a legitimate part of God's people. Paul wrote to assure them that they were (9:24-29; 10:6-13; 11:22-24). The issue was not whether Jews were a part of God's people. The question was whether Gentile Christians were included. And

third, after Paul wrestled with this matter for a long time, he finally concluded that the whole issue remained a mystery, locked in the inscrutable ways and unsearchable judgments of God. (11:33-36)[52]

David Gill offered an enlightening view of this Pauline thought when he wrote that "spiritual gifts" can in fact also be translated as "spiritual people."[53] Gill seemed to point out that there were two classifications of people: those who believed in Jesus' humanity and deity and those who denied His humanity but believed in His deity.

Crucial Word Studies

Considering all the irregularities in the Corinthian church, Paul turned his teaching toward the use of spiritual gifts something I also endeavored to do in and through this project. Paul was clear to address the spiritual gifts and not the spiritual people. According to Strong's Concordance, and is translated "Holy Spirit."[54] Paul recalled the time when the Gentiles were carried away and led astray by idols, but he wanted them to know the difference between idol spirits and the Holy Spirit.

Paul seemed to be clear in his directive to focus on unity as opposed to a hierarchy of gifts. Paul stated, "No man speaking by the Spirit of God calleth Jesus accursed" (1 Corinthians 12:3). David Nichols believed "in this context that it is difficult saying (Jesus be cursed) is an actual statement which the Corinthians claimed they could say based on their present eschatological existence."[55] Nichols further believes that this was done by the same Corinthians who saw no sin in mingling with prostitutes in the temple. Gnosticism, a belief in special, extra-biblical revelation available to a chosen

---

[52]W. Eugene March, *Great Themes of the Bible*, vol. 1 (Lousville, KY: Westminister John Knox, 2007), 108.

[53]David Gill, *Romans to Philemon*, Zondervan Illustrated Bible Backgrounds Commentary, vol. 3, Clinton E. Arnold, ed. (Grand Rapids, MI: Zondervan, 1984), 163.

[54]Archibald T Robertson, *Epistles of Paul*, Word Pictures in The New Testament, vol. 4 (Nashville, TN: Broadman, 1931), 167.

[55]David R. Nichols, "The Problem of Two-Level Christianity at Corinth," *Pneuma* 7, no. 2 (1989): 106.

few has received the blame for most of this behavior.

Archibald Robertson defined the word *accursed* (*anathema*) in the Greek to mean "a thing devoted to God without being redeemed, doomed to destruction."[56] Therefore Paul stated, "If any man love not the Lord Jesus Christ, let him be anathema Maranatha" (1 Corinthians 16:22). Paul was quite clear in his counsel that all were to be accursed who did not love the Lord because Jesus is Lord. The Aramaic phrase *Maranatha* means "Our Lord" (*maran*) cometh (*atha*)" or, used as a proleptic perfect, "has come."[57] Paul wanted the Corinthians to know that Jesus is Lord. However, this word Lord was used both by the cult of Christ and the cult of Caesar and there could not be two Lords. Lord in the Greek is translated as *kurios*. It was believed that the emperor deserved the honor of being called lord but Paul denied that and stated there is only one Lord, which is Jesus Christ.

Paul sought to address the gifts in verse four and added that there are diversities or varieties of gifts but the same Spirit. "Diversities in the Greek is (*diaireseis*) which is an old word for distinctions, differences, distributions, from *diaireo*, to distribute, as *diairoun* (dividing, distributing) in verse 11."[58] Paul further expressed that, through the diversity of gifts, there are differences of administrations and diversity of operations; however, they all come from one source.

Paul declared that this source was through the same Lord, same God, and the same Spirit. Here, the Trinitarian Godhead was displayed as the unifying agent for all the gifts. Robertson suggested,

> The ministrations (*diakonion*) has a general meaning of service as here (Romans 11:13) and a special ministration like that of Martha (Luke 10:40) and the collection (1 Corinthians 16:15; 2 Corinthians.8:4). Of workings (*energematon*). Late word, here only N.T., the effect of a thing wrought (from *energeo*, to operate, perform, energize). Paul

---

[56]Robertson, 167.
[57]Robertson, 204.
[58]Robertson, 168.

uses also the late kindred word *energeia* (Colossians 1:29; 2:12) for efficiency. Paul is not afraid to say that God is the Energy and the Energizer of the Universe. Manifestation (*phanerosis*). Last word, in papyri, in N.T. only here and II Cor. 4:2, from *phaneroo*, to make manifest (*phaneros*).[59]

Theological Interpretation: Status and Conduct of the Corinthians

David Nichols raises questions if Paul was dealing with spiritual things or spiritual persons. It seems Paul was dealing with people because in verse two, it is clear he addressed the Corinthians' former existence as Gentiles. Paul was concerned with their conduct and described how one should carry oneself as a believer. Nichols believes, "The entire discussion of spiritual gifts is set in the context of the realized eschatology embraced by the Corinthians. This eschatology caused them to think that they were above sin and evil, no matter what they did with their bodies."[60] However, to their surprise, this type of behavior not only caused problems but severed the relationship between them and the Lord Jesus Christ. Gary Charles suggests,

> In verses 1-3 Paul warns that not all ecstatic expression is charismatic and in verse 4-13 that not all charismatic expression is ecstatic. There is a criterion for assessing charismatic expression that is more significant than one's own spiritual experience. Both faith and the charismatic expression of faith are Spirit-given possibilities. Therefore, ecstatic behavior is not necessarily charismatic, unless it bears witness to the lordship of Jesus Christ. Conversely, no charismatic behavior is genuine unless it does the same. Paul's initial comment in this chapter set the tone for the remaining verses. They serve to caution Christians who too easily devalue their gifts, reminding them that faith itself comes as a God-given gift. They also caution

---

[59]Robertson, 168-169.
[60]Nichols, 106.

Christians too confident of their own spiritual status that faith came to them as a gracious gift, not of their own making.[61]

Charles is clear regarding the status of Christians who acted like the Corinthians. The idea is reinforced by the fact that all comes from God and Christians have no meaning or identity unless they are unified with Jesus Christ. It was logical and an extension of Paul's teaching that even though the Corinthians had all the spiritual gifts in operation, their behavior was in danger of rendering them renegades in their moral rebellion against the Lordship of Christ.

Craig Keener seems to be in agreement with Charles and Nichols in that "Paul indicates that prophesying is not necessarily a sign of godliness; pagans prophesied, too, and at Greek oracular shrines possessed persons prophesied ecstatically, inspired by gods other than the Christian God."[62] Keener further suggests that Paul was clear in relating to the Corinthians that former behavior in paganism and ecstatic action did not constitute godly attributes.

Maybe it is here that Paul chose to refresh the Corinthians' memory of where they had come from as Gentiles and that Jesus Christ was then the unifying source of their spiritual gifts. Craig states "that manifestations of the Spirit are to be found in wide varieties of conduct, because spirituality exists wherever the living, acting God works through capacities of any type. Spirituality is not a separate compartment of life, but a divine relationship which may enable all aspects of experience."[63] In other words, their spiritual gifts were to reflect a holy life and were not an indication that holiness was irrelevant to the Lord.

Diversity of Spiritual Gifts

In 1 Corinthians 12:4, Paul addressed the diversity of the gifts. John Walvoord wrote, "Spiritual gifts are divinely

---

[61] Gary W. Charles, "1 Corinthians 12:1-13," *Charisma: Peer Reviewed, Interpretation* 44, no. 1 (1990): 66.

[62] Craig S. Keener, *New Testament, The IVP Bible Background Commentary* (Downers Grove, IL: InterVarsity, 1993), 478.

[63] Craig, 149.

given capacities to perform useful functions for God, especially in the area of spiritual service."[64] Paul affirmed this truth and reiterated that the diversity of spiritual gifts operated only through the unified Godhead. Paul was clear in his language that the sources of these gifts are the same Lord, same God, and the same Spirit.

Craig explains, "From the same 'Spirit,' 'Lord,' "and 'God' come the means for the church to carry out its function through gifts, service, and working."[65] Pagans might consider what they could do for the deity through sacrifices and the dedication of gifts, but Paul was clear to say in Christian terms that favor with God, as evidenced by the spiritual gifts being given to the Body, is through God, the Holy Spirit, and Jesus Christ. The Holy Spirit gives a diversity of gifts so individuals can serve the Lord and His body, the Church, in various ways, and all are empowered by God and are exercised under His direction. Though there are different kinds of gifts, services, and workings, the same Spirit, the same Lord, and the same God are involved in all of them.

Paul composed a list of these gifts where God gives believers a word, wisdom, and knowledge. Keener suggests that these refer to God giving the ability for one to speak and teach. Keener further asserts that these impart the ability to speak supernaturally.

The Big Question: Are Spiritual Gifts for Today?

Charles delivers a modern perspective of spiritual gifts in the local church. He affirms that the diversity of gifts in the Corinthian church resulted in disunity and further suggests that this problem stemmed from a life centered around inappropriate hierarchy among the leadership. This is the reason Paul was so persistent in his argument that all spiritual gifts came from God and are to bear witness of Jesus Christ. Charles suggests, "This text's [1 Corinthians 12] emphasis on

---

[64] John F. Walvoord, "The Holy Spirit and Spiritual Gifts," *Bibliotheca Sacra* 143, no. 570 (1986): 109. *ATLA Religion Database,* EBSCOhost (17 March 2013).

[65] Craig, 164.

gifts given for the common good warrants a fresh reading by the modern church."[66]

Today when the sociological and cultural climate fosters individualism, the church is placed in a precarious state for no member has all that he or she needs to grow spiritually. We need the teaching, prophetic, or faith gifts that others have, which were given by the Spirit according to His will and purpose. The Church should be able to offer a new experience when members choose to embrace the diversity of gifts.

Charles is of the opinion that this marriage between individualism and spiritual gifts may foster church growth as opposed to utilizing gimmicks in the application of evangelism, concluding once again that 1 Corinthians 12 is vital for the Church today:

> In 1 Corinthians 12:1-13 Paul states his understanding of a genuinely charismatic church. First, a charismatic church recognizes that the gifts of God's Spirit are given to every Christian, not just to a fortunate few. Secondly, charismatic Christianity accepts spiritual gifts for practical use and ministry, not simply for display. Finally, the truly charismatic church knows that Christian unity is not a personal achievement but a remarkable gift from God. To treat this text seriously invites the church to reclaim its God-given character. Gifted and nurtured by God's Spirit, the church exists neither to enable Christians to reach the heights of ecstatic spiritual experience nor simply to bless the piety. The church exists to glorify Jesus as its Lord, to live by God's life-giving Spirit, and to invite all Christians to express their gifts in the way in which they were intended—for the common good.[67]

As general editor of *Are Miraculous Gifts for Today*, Wayne Grudem presents four major views regarding the significance of vocal spiritual gifts in today's world.[68] Grudem

---

[66]Charles, 67.

[67]Charles, 68.

[68]Wayne A. Grudem, ed., *Are Miraculous Gifts For Today? Four Views* (Grand Rapids, MI: Zondervan, 1996), 10-12.

attempted to answer many questions on the table regarding spiritual gifts and their operation in the modern church. He asserts what we already know—that there are many differences among believers over specific spiritual gifts.[69] Grudem further contrasted Pentecostals, who believe that Christians should seek to be baptized in the Holy Spirit after conversion, with evangelicals who maintain that they have been baptized in the Holy Spirit at the moment they are converted. I will examine at this issue more closely in a later chapter regarding Grudem's position regarding vocal spiritual gifts.

---

[69]Grudem, 9.

CHAPTER 5

THE CESSATIONIST VIEW

This is really the crux of the entire matter concerning spiritual gifts. There are some who believe the gifts still operate and function today while another group, called cessationists, believe the gifts pretty much ceased to exist when the last of the original apostles died. The gifts ceased, according to them, which is where they got their name. Let's look at what some others had to say that have influenced my thinking where this issue is concerned.

Richard B. Gaffin Jr. suggests that the cessationist views the work of the Holy Spirit as "tied up in a tidy, comfortable little package."[70] Therefore, cessationists have chosen to compromise the power of the Holy Spirit and it grieves the Holy Spirit.[71] Cessationists have argued against the theology presented and the picture painted by Luke. Grudem further explains that the term "history of salvation" refers to the finished work of Christ and none of the works of Christ are repeatable; however, the term "order of salvation" represents the continuing works of Christ in the lives of individuals throughout

---

[70] Richard B. Gaffin Jr, "Cessationist," *Are Miraculous Gifts For Today? Four Views*, in Wayne Grudem ed. (Grand Rapids, MI: Zondervan, 1996), 25.

[71] Gaffin, 27.

history.[72] Let's look at the history and the order of salvation for a moment. "These two are the part of Christ's once-for-all accomplishment of His work of earning our salvation."[73]

Pentecost in the minds of the cessationist is a one-of-a-kind act and is not repeatable. If one event is repeatable, then the event of Jesus' resurrection and ascension should be repeatable.[74] Cessationists further believe that one receives everything they need upon conversion.[75] Pentecost is redemptive-historical and Christological and not experiential. Acts 1:8 illustrates that there was a subsequent event to take place after salvation. This passage shows that there was one more event necessary in order for believers to be empowered to be witnesses for Christ. This out-of-the-box experience was to empower the believer for service. Pentecost may not be repeatable, but the second infilling experience is repeatable for the continuation for the ministry of Jesus Christ. Luke was clear in his narrative that there is a subsequent experience following conversion.

An Open but Cautious View

Many authors and commentators have created misunderstanding and doubt concerning the gifts when they claim there are no biblical commands existing to be baptized with the Spirit or to receive the Spirit in a new way. One such author states that there are two commands in the Bible concerning the Spirit: one is to live by the Spirit (see Galatians 5:16, 25) and the other is to be filled with the Spirit (see Ephesians 5:18).[76] These two commands may be weak theology in the minds of a cessationist but these verses accurately describe Pentecostal theology. Saucy seems to embrace the theology of cessationalism that miracles and spiritual gifts ceased to operate at the end of the apostolic era.

---

[72] Grudem, 31.
[73] Gaffin, 31.
[74] Gaffin, 33.
[75] Gaffin, 34.
[76] Robert L. Saucy, "Open But Cautious," in *Are Miraculous Gifts For Today? Four Views*, Wayne Grudem ed. (Grand Rapids, MI: Zondervan, 1996), 98.

He believes that signs and miracles followed the lives of the apostles, but since the apostles passed on, the miraculous gifts did not remain in operation. He also notes that these signs are not biblically attached to every individual who spoke and taught the word of God.[77] The author emphasizes that Scripture is clear that signs and wonders followed those whose ministries were at crucial turning points.[78] Of course I challenge and disagree with this view based on my own study, interpretation of Scripture, and personal experience. What's more, I believe struggling and dying churches are in desperate need of the Spirit, which is why I embarked on this journey for my DMin project and in my church.

God is not in a box and is not restricted by rules or human preferences. Believers must follow Paul's exhortation to test God in everything (see 1Thessalonians 5:21). According to Scripture, spiritual gifts were vital to the life and growth of the church in Acts so why would we assume that would change for the modern church? Are our needs any less? Has the way God has chosen to reach people and cause the church to grow changed? Church history is good to learn and learn from, but God wants His people to come in the knowledge of *biblical* truth. Saucy is clear on this point that all of God's people have gifts and I agree.[79]

Therefore, the apostles' work has not ceased and the canons have not been closed (by that I mean that the effectiveness of Scripture to touch people has not diminished nor has the Spirit's desire to touch His people through the Spirit). Ephesians 4 is clear as to how God intends to equip His church (the work of apostles, prophets, evangelists, pastor, and teachers), and we need to seek God more to bring forth the modern apostolic anointing so signs and wonders may follow.

Third Wave Christians have a similarity with classical Pentecostals but differ in the subsequent theory. "Third Wave Christians believe that Spirit Baptism is an event subsequent to and therefore separate from the reception of the

---

[77] Saucy, 106.
[78] Saucy, 108.
[79] Saucy, 141.

Spirit at conversion, the initial evidence of which is speaking in tongues."[80] However, there may be multiple experiences after conversion. These multiple experiences are to be related to what the New Testament calls the "filling" of the Spirit. John Wimber was an advocate of this view.

Wimber suggested that Spirit baptism comes at conversion: "Conversion and Holy Spirit Baptism are simultaneous experiences."[81] Storms adds that evangelicals are right in affirming that all Christians are baptized in the Spirit at conversion but wrong denying the subsequent experiences.[82] Charismatics are right in affirming the reality of post-conversion experiences but are wrong in calling them Spirit baptism. Cessationists do not deny the ability of miraculous works occurring subsequent to the death of the apostles; they choose to deny post-apostolic operation of the revelatory gifts such as tongues, prophecy, interpretation of tongues, and miracles.[83] The cessationists also believe that one who exercises the gift of healing or the gift of miracles can exercise supernatural power at will and have the same effect as the apostles.[84]

According to Samuel Storms, Charles Spurgeon came to the conclusion through personal experience that the gifts of the Spirit are for the church today, primarily because the Bible gives no evidence to the contrary. The purpose of the gifts is to build up the body of Christ, and the Bible is clear that these gifts are to be operative until the return of our Lord.[85] D. A. Carson states, "The coming of the Spirit is not associated merely with the dawning of the new age but with its presence, not merely with Pentecost, but with the entire period from Pentecost to the return of Jesus the Messiah."[86]

"Pentecostals believe the 'receiving' of the Spirit is a

---

[80] C. Samuel Storms, "Third Wave," in *Are Miraculous Gifts For Today? Four Views*, Wayne Grudem ed. (Grand Rapids, MI: Zondervan, 1996), 176.
[81] Storms, 176.
[82] Storms, 179.
[83] Storms, 185.
[84] Storms, 186.
[85] Storms, 205.
[86] Storms, 206.

post-conversion experience when the Spirit empowers the believer in charismatic ways for service."[87] This experience can happen immediately upon conversion without any time lapse. Pentecostals do not see this experience as a once-and-for-all event. It's their belief that there is an ongoing refilling of the Holy Spirit to repeat the work. Douglas A. Oss states, "Baptism in the Holy Spirit, as Pentecostals have defined it in their systemic theology, is the first experience of the Spirit's empowering work, which inaugurates a life characterized by continued anointing with the Spirit."[88] Thus, the ongoing presence and infilling of the Spirit is vital if the church and its members are to fulfill their God-given purpose to grow and to reach the world with the gospel of Christ.

Carson evaluated Ron Stronstadt's approach to the distinction between Pauline and Lukan pneumatologies (theology of the Holy Spirit). These theologies differ in that classical Pentecostals include in their theology that there is a secondary post-conversion experience that empowers the believer for service. The Pauline approach distinctly looks at the baptism into one Spirit [body]. The Pauline text allows one to believe that all is achieved at conversion while Luke emphasizes the empowering work of the Spirit rather than inner transformation. While the Pauline text deals primarily with a problematic audience, Lukan pneumatology presents a work of the Holy Spirit distinct from salvation.

Classical Pentecostalism is strongly supported throughout the Bible to illustrate that when the Spirit came upon prophets and others, Spirit-prompted speech was the result.[89] Jack Deere writes that cessationism originated in experience, and the lack of experience has caused cessationists to view miracles and gifts as temporary endowments no longer expected in church.[90]

---

[87]Douglas A. Oss, "Pentecostal/Charismatic," *Are Miraculous Gifts For Today?: Four Views*, Wayne Grudem ed. (Grand Rapids, MI: Zondervan, 1996), 242.

[88]Oss, 243.

[89]Oss, 250.

[90]Jack Deere, *Surprised By The Power Of The Spirit* (Grand Rapids, MI: Zondervan, 1993) 100.

Ecclesiological (theology of the Church) Views

Paul explained in 1 Corinthians that there were contentions in the Body at Corinth that were heating up and causing friction. David Ackerman insightfully states, "Friction can be a good thing when it sharpens dull edges, but if allowed to progress unchecked, it can create excessive heat, eventually igniting a fire."[91] Ackerman further alludes to the fact that all the ingredients were present to start a fire, but the church had not yet burst into flames. Paul was obviously concerned with the level of spiritual immaturity in the body. In 1 Corinthians 12-14, Paul addressed spiritual matters.

David Ackerman suggests that the Corinthians classified themselves as mature because they possessed certain gifts of the Spirit. However, their abuse and misuse of these gifts heightened friction in the church. Paul's goal in these chapters, therefore, was to free the Corinthians from their ignorance of spiritual matters.

Ackerman explains, "Paul goes on to condemn their wrong interpretation of spirituality. Gifts of the Spirit can be wonderful tools for the church if put through the filter of the cross, but if used in self-service, they can become the fuel for a fiery demise."[92] Author Ronald Fung shares that the gifts of the Spirit may be thought of as gifts of the exalted Christ.[93] I see the common ground shared by Ackerman and Fung in that these spiritual gifts are prompted through Christ and should be used under the direction of Christ.

However, the real issue in the Corinthian church through the lens of Paul was spiritual immaturity. So, Paul addressed the church concerning what it meant to be spiritual by addressing spiritual gifts. "The word *charismata* basically denotes the manifestation of *charis* or grace. Paul states, 'But one and the same Spirit works all these things, distributing to

---

[91] David A. Ackerman, "Fighting Fire with Fire: Community Formation in 1 Corinthians 12-14," *Evangelical Review of Theology* 29, no. 4 (October 2005): 347.

[92] Ackerman, 349.

[93] Ronald Y. K. Fung, "Ministry, Community and Spiritual Gifts," *The Evangelical Quarterly* (1984): 7.

each one individually just as He wills" (1 Corinthians 12:11). It is God who gives this charisma to whom He pleases. This is a uniquely Pauline word, with half of all uses of the term occurring in 1 Corinthians."[94] Fung insightfully states, "A charisma then is a grace gift, a free gift which has its source in and is an expression of God's grace."[95]

"Charisma and *diakonia* or service are related concepts. *Diakonia* is rooted in charisma, since every *diakonia* in the church presupposes the call of God. Charisma leads to *diakonia* since every charisma in the church only finds fulfillment in service. Where there is a real charisma, there will be responsible service for the edification and benefit of the community."[96] Fung acknowledges that gifts in the church isolated from the giver lose the character of the Lord Jesus Christ. To have the ability to edify the community, spiritual gifts are employed through the power and confession of the Lord Jesus Christ.

Fung concludes that Paul had a balanced doctrine of the inner nature of the ministry, as well as the doctrines of the church and the charismata. This doctrine of the ministry is aligned with Paul's ecclesiology and charisma-tology and is found to be connected by three vital principles: the headship of Christ, the growth of the Body, and unity and multiplicity.[97] "Furthermore, in view of the fact that much of Paul's doctrine of the ministry is explicable in terms of his conception of the Church as the Body of Christ and his conception of spiritual gifts, his doctrine of the ministry may be regarded as largely consequent upon his ecclesiology and his charismatology."[98]

Let me say that from this point forward, I get a bit more technical, drawing once again on my research I did for my DMin project. I am not trying to impress you, nor do I expect you to do what I did. However, I hope you will take these lessons with you as you read and then reflect on how to apply what I have written.

---

[94] Ackerman, 350.
[95] Fung, 5.
[96] Fung, 7.
[97] Fung, 18.
[98] Fung, 18.

1. It's time to do an assessment in your church (or to conduct one personally).
2. How can you measure where the people are at spiritually?
3. What teaching can you do outside of Sunday morning to equip the people to be more engaged with the Lord?
4. What can you do to assist people who want to identify and use their spiritual gifts?
5. After your teaching, how will you measure whether or not the effort was fruitful?

I will do more teaching in the next few chapters, for that was what I did in my church. I taught the people what I saw in God's Word. Having said that, let's move on to further discuss spiritual gifts and their relevance for the church today.

CHAPTER 6

THE SEMINAR

I have given you all the philosophical and theological background needed at this point and now I want to share with you what I taught in the workshops that were designed to equip the members of my congregation for greater awareness and use of spiritual gifts in our congregation.

SESSION ONE

Introduction

The first class session began by handing out packets to all the participants consisting of pre-class and post-class surveys along with the lecture notes. The pre-class and post-class surveys consisting of twenty-five questions—five questions addressed per class session. After the pre-class survey, I asked the participants to discuss the question "Are vocal spiritual gifts significant?" and gave them fifteen minutes to interact with one another. This cultivated and stimulated a greater interest in the knowledge of vocal spiritual gifts as the groups got to hear from one another, some of whom (like me) who had experience with those gifts that others had not. Here is a summary of what each group's findings.

Group A

Vocal spiritual gifts are significant because they edify the whole spirit of man. This enhancement culminates in a greater sensitivity when communing with the person of the Holy Spirit. The question that surfaced during our discussion about the African American Baptist Church is, "Why did Jesus not teach on vocal spiritual gifts"? We then determined that in fact He did. Jesus stated, "And these signs will accompany those who have believed: in My name they will cast out demons, they will speak with new tongues" (Mark 16:17). Then we found cross-references to Acts 2:4 and I Corinthians 12: 28 that relate to the passage from Mark 16. The Greek word for *tongues* is *glossa*, which can also be interpreted as *language*. Language here is a dialect that is different from one's native language. It is a supernatural utterance and an unknown dialect that is not understood by man but is known only to God.

Group B

Christians are involved in spiritual warfare: "For our struggle is not against flesh and blood, but against the rulers, against the powers, against the world forces of this darkness, against the spiritual forces of wickedness in the heavenly places" (Eph 6:12). This battle can neither be fought nor conquered through carnal weapons. Christian weapons must be spiritual. Paul declares, 'For the weapons of our warfare are not of the flesh, but divinely powerful for the destruction of fortresses" (2 Corinthians 10:4). We need the spiritual gifts so we have all the weapons we need to fight the good fight of faith.

Sections 4 A-B

Tongues, the interpretation of tongues, and prophecy all bestow personal benefits. Tongues edify the whole spirit of man. Paul admonishes, "One who speaks in a tongue edifies himself; but one who prophesies edifies the church" (l Corinthians 14:4). Which one is more important? Both are equally important, because in private devotion man's inner being, his spirit, needs to be spiritually uplifted. In the public setting, the church needs to be instructed and spiritually uplifted. However, tongues given in the public setting have to interpreted. In other words, the spiritual utterance that is given from God to man has to be interpreted into a known dialect for the church to understand. This subject will be covered more in depth in the next section.

Section 4C

In this chapter, three Old Testament passages will be

examined, helping you to see how significant vocal spiritual gifts are and the importance of them being manifested. The Old Testament mainly illustrates God speaking directly to man in a known dialect. This known dialect was classified as prophecy.

Moses (Numbers 11)

In Numbers 11, it is noted that Moses was in charge of the children of Israel enroute to the promised land. The children of Israel begin to complain about their food situation. Constant complaining became burdensome to Moses. Moses began himself to complain to God and wanted to blame God for placing the welfare and responsibility of all the people on his shoulders. God heard Moses and commanded him to find seventy from the elders of Israel. God promised Moses that he would not have to bear the responsibility alone.

God stated to Moses, "Consecrate yourselves for tomorrow, and you shall eat meat; for you have wept in the ears of the Lord, saying, "Oh that someone would give us meat to eat! For we were well off in Egypt." Therefore, the Lord will give you meat and you shall eat" (Numbers 11:18). The Lord supplied Israel with meat to eat for a month, and they ate until it ran from their nostrils because Israel had rejected the Lord. Moses continued to question God and His ability to supply meat for the six hundred thousand people. The Lord exclaims, "Is the Lord's power limited? Now you shall see whether My word will come true for you or not" (Numbers 11:23).

Moses went out and told the word of the Lord to the people, and he gathered seventy men of Israel. God formed a wind that brought quail from the seas and let them fall all around the camp. Quails fell thirty-six inches deep (two cubits) on the ground. The people of Israel gathered quail day and night and all the next day.

Ezekiel (Ezekiel 37: 1—14)

The second Old Testament prophet to be considered is Ezekiel. We looked at some of this previously, but let me repeat it here for emphasis. "Ezekiel was a prophet of a priestly family carried captive to Babylon in 597 B.C. Ezekiel prophesied to the captives who dwelt by the River Chebar at Tel Abib."[99] Ezekiel 37 reveals the prophetic work of God. God uses His prophet Ezekiel to speak a word to a useless nation to revitalize them with the hope of His spoken word. Ralph H. Alexander explains, "Chapter 37 begins without any transition, simply revealing the apocalyptic vision that concluded Ezekiel's message on Israel's future restoration. This vision pictures the manner in which the Lord would restore His people."[100] Alexander is of the opinion that this event did not really take place but rather was a vision given to Ezekiel to symbolize Israel's future restoration.

The vision took place in the valley of the Euphrates River in Babylon. Scholars believe that this is the same valley mentioned in Ezekiel. The valley was full of dried, sun-parched, good-for-nothing bones. Blenkinsopp comments, "'The hand of Yahweh was upon me,' indicating the state of trance in which the vision was experienced."[101] The Bible suggests that Ezekiel was in the Spirit when he was led into the valley. God addressed Ezekiel with a question and asked, 'Can these bones live?"

Ezekiel was wise in that he chose not to answer God; he knew the power of God extended even into the realm of death. Hall explains, 'The prophet answered the challenge to faith by saying that his faith was small, but that the God of his faith was great."[102] God commanded Ezekiel to prophesy over the bones. The prophecy was plain and simple. "O dry bones, hear the word of the Lord" (v. 4). Prophecy is bringing the Word of God to the problems of people. According to Hall, 'Prophecy is not only a foretelling but rather a forth telling."[103]

Ezekiel brought forth the Word of God to the dried bones to resurrect their lives from their graves of hopelessness.

---

[99] Youngblood, 'Moses," 429.

[100] Ralph H. Alexander, *Ezekiel: The Expositor's Bible Commentary*, vol. 6, ed. Frank Gaebelein (Grands Rapids, MI: Zondervan, 1990), 924.

[101] Joseph Blenkinsopp, *Ezekiel: Interpretation Bible Commentary*, ed. James Luther Mays (Louisville, KY: John Knox, 1990), 170.

[102] Bert H. Hall, *Jeremiah, Lamentations, Ezekiel, and Daniel: The Wesleyan Bible Commentary*, vol. 3 (Peabody, MA: Hendrickson, 1979), 467.

[103] Hall, 467.

Ezekiel records, "Behold, I will cause breath to enter you that you may come to life. And I will put sinews on you, make flesh grow back on you, cover you with skin, and put breath in you that you may come alive; and you will know that I am the Lord" (vs. 5-6). The Bible bears witness that Ezekiel obeyed God, and immediately there was a rattling noise. Hall notes, "The Hebrew may be translated literally, 'and there was a voice, as I prophesied, and, lo, a rustling, and the bones come together.'"[104] As Ezekiel prophesied, the voice of God was heard and made the bones tremble and shake.

The Bible illustrates that two stages of life are evident. Ezekiel prophesied the first time, and God clothed the bones with sinews, muscles, and tendons. The second prophecy gave breath, or the Spirit of God, to the lifeless bodies to re-establish life. The infallible Word of God is clear in that when the Spirit of God entered the lifeless bodies, they all stood on their feet as a great army. Blenkinsopp asserts, "It is the Spirit-activated prophetic preaching which bonds the community together and gives it the will to live and accept its future."[105]

The Spirit of God directed Ezekiel, in a vision, to the middle of a valley. This valley was full of bones, which represented the nation of Israel. God chose sun-parched, dried bones that seemed to have been there for a long period of time. God commanded Ezekiel to prophesy to the bones. It was only through the proclamation of the prophecy that the bones were to receive flesh and be resurrected, so God commanded Ezekiel to prophesy to the winds to cause His Spirit to enter the bodies, and then they became living souls. The text then declares that the bodies of the people stood on their feet as a great army. Ezekiel's to God revealed that through the assertion of prophecy, humankind is resurrected from the state of being hopeless. Life is sustained through the word and Spirit of God.

Joel (Joel 2:28)

The last Old Testament prophet to be considered is

---

[104]Hall, 467.
[105]Blenkinsopp, 173.

Joel. The Book of Joel is explicit in detailing the plague of locusts that devastated the land and depleted all agricultural resources. "What the gnawing locust has left, the swarming locust has eaten; And what the swarming locust has left, the creeping locust has eaten; And what the creeping locust has left, the stripping locust has eaten" (Joel 1:4). According to Linburg, "To the prophet, the 'day of the Lord' was near (1:15; 2:1)."[106] Linburg notes that the "day of the Lord" is a time in which God will intervene in history.[107] Joel refers to this event twice in chapters one and two. The Babylonian army destroyed Jerusalem in 586 BC. Linburg observes, "Along with the notion that the Day of the Lord means salvation for Israel goes the idea of doom for Israel's enemies."[108]

God speaks to the prophet Joel to call for a return to Him. Linburg suggests that Israel had fallen away from God, and through this falling away God allowed devastation to come to the people and the land.[109] God commands Joel to tell the people to "consecrate a fast" (1:14). If the people chose not to return to God, they would have to suffer the terrible Day of the Lord. The people were familiar with the traditional practices of fasting. Linburg elaborates, "How should a people return to the Lord? Joel 2:12-13 frames the traditional practices of fasting with the assertion that a true return to the Lord is a matter of the heart."[110] Joel is clear in communicating to the people why they should return to the Lord, Joel 2:13 states that God is gracious, compassionate, slow to anger, and abounding in love.

God refreshes the call to Joel in 2:15 to "blow the trumpet and consecrate a fast." God instructed Joel to gather the people. "Spare thy people, O Lord" (Joel 2:17). This is the cry that God gave to Joel to communicate to the people of God. Obedience to this prophetic message would cause the

---

[106] James Linburg, *Hosea-Micah*, Interpretation Commentary (Atlanta, GA: John Knox, 1988), 63.
[107] Linburg, 63.
[108] Linburg, 64.
[109] Linburg, 64.
[110] Linburg, 66.

all-loving, most gracious, and slow-to-anger God to initiate deliverance. All that had been devastated and condemned would be restored and forgiven.

Joel continued this prophetic message to allow the people to know, "You shall have plenty to eat and be satisfied. And praise the name of the Lord your God, who dealt wondrously with you; then my people will never be put to shame" (2:26). God is clear through these signs and wonders of replenishment that He is the God of His Word and beside Him there is no other (verse 27). Faith in Israel's God brings deliverance from judgment.

Richard Patterson observes, "These chapters disclose the Lord's eschatological intentions. Two primary thoughts are included: the Lord's promise of personal provision in the lives of His own (2:28-32) and the prediction of His final triumph on behalf of His own at the culmination of the history of mankind."[111] Joel points out that the intent of the Lord is to pour out His Spirit on all flesh (v. 28). This was not to be an impartation to selected individuals but to male and female, old and young. John Thompson suggests.

"All flesh could mean all mankind, as in Isaiah 40:5, but the following possessives (your sons and daughters, etc.) show that the phrase here means all Israel. Previously, the spirit of prophecy had been limited to a chosen few, but under this new dispensation God's revelation would come to both male and female, to both old and young, and even to the servant class."[112] A renewed spiritual encounter would encompass prophesying, dreams, and visions.

According to the prophetic message of Joel, there had to be a return to the Lord through the hearts of humankind before the Lord chose to pour out His Spirit. It was to be after the return to God that people would be enabled to have the

---

[111] Richard Patterson, *Daniel-Minor Prophets: The Expositor's Bible Commentary*, vol. 7, ed. Frank Gaebelein (Grand Rapids, MI: Zondervan, 1990), 255.

[112] John Thompson, *Lamentations-Ezekiel-Daniel and Twelve Prophets: The Interpreter's Bible*, vol 6, George A Buttrick, ed. (Nashville, TN: Abingdon, 1956), 752.

impartation of the Holy Spirit. John Thompson also asserts that the gift of prophecy enabled the prophets and those in the future to have the ability to discern and declare the will of God.[113]

It was in Ezekiel's vision that the Spirit of God gave life to the dried bones. Linburg concludes, "To receive the Spirit is to receive power, which can manifest itself both in acts (mighty deeds) and words (prophecy)."[114] Prophecy, dreams, and visions are all biblical means of the revelation of God.

Summary

Three distinct spiritual gifts have been researched in this project and I inserted various positions from known theologians to give you an idea of how some have interpreted issues outside of Baptist tradition. Variations may be observed from different platforms; however, there are many similarities. I chose to look at the gift of tongues, the interpretation of tongues, and the gift of prophecy or what I termed the vocal spiritual gifts. Biblically, tongues are seen to be in two distinct practices, the tongues of prayer and the gift of tongues.

Oral Roberts classified tongues as one's prayer language. This is where Christians do not know what they are saying. It is suggested that these utterances or groans are offered up to God as divine communication with Him. Only God can understand these words of divine utterance. Christians are encouraged to do this in private because unbelievers may see people so engaged as a bit off or crazy. However, the gift of tongues differs in that the tongue may be given in the corporate setting and then another (or even the same person who uttered the tongues) will receive an interpretation. Paul suggested that this gift is a sign for the unbeliever but that there must be an interpreter. The sole purpose of the gift of tongues is to edify or encourage the congregation.

Paul further noted that if there is no interpreter, the speaker must keep silent. Also, Paul encourages the speaker to pray to God for the gift of interpretation. Some have found

---

[113] Thompson, 752.
[114] Linburg, 71.

it difficult to speak in tongues or even possess the gift of tongues. Roberts suggested that if one would pray unto God and then just open one's mouth and begin to speak in English, God will enable that person to speak. There has been much scrutiny of this matter, and consequently the frequency of tongues has greatly diminished in the church. Many churches have chosen to neglect the practice of tongues because they believe that tongues, interpretation Of tongues, and prophecy ceased with the apostles. Some of the theologians have taken the position that these gifts are finding their way back in the church due to teaching and increasing the knowledge of the church.

A number of the theologians researched in this project have suggested that the interpretation of tongues is closely associated with the gift of prophecy. This is mainly due to the fact that the revelation of the interpretation comes directly from God. This is not something that people can dream up or create from their own intellect. Tongues are spoken vertically unto God and God speaks directly unto man that man may speak the message of God horizontally unto the church. This biblical formula is seen to edify the church. Furthermore, if an unbeliever comes in the church and observe the gift of tongues being spoken and hear the interpretation, they will not deem people as being crazy.

My own position throughout this book has been that the church today—*all* churches—need all the spiritual help we can get and the spiritual gifts are the help we need. God knows how to build and care for His church and spiritual gifts are a part of His plan. When we ignore them, we then try to use other means to do the work that only God can do where church growth and nurture are concerned.

The research from my Doctor of Ministry project showed that with just a little training, members in a congregation will better understand and be less intimidated by the thought of spiritual gifts, thus flowing in them more freely. Then others will be more comfortable with their use and God can prove to His people that He is alive, well, and willing to speak to them not only through the pulpit but also through one another. Of course, we have mostly examined the vocal gifts, but the other gifts mentioned in 1 Corinthians 12, 1 Peter 4, and Romans 12 are also necessary for the church to flow and grow in the Spirit. I will leave that discussion for another time and place. Let me make some concluding thoughts in the next few pages as we close out this look at my research and conclusions on the gifts, church growth, and the role of teaching in the life of every local congregation.

FINAL THOUGHTS

Thank you persevering with me in reading through some of my dissertation. It brought back a lot of memories, both good and painful, but it reminded me how far I have come in the last ten years since I wrote this. I have been a pastor through the pandemic and now my focus is even more singular since my other employment has ceased. I am teaching even more classes than before at Southwestern Christian University and I have had even more time to think through and apply what I believe where spiritual gifts and church growth are concerned. I have a friend who wrote a book titled *Changing the Way We Do Church*. I have become more and more convinced of that reality if we are serious about having an impact in modern life.

When I used to consider the word or title *pastor*, I thought it represented the work of an overseer in a church. He (or perhaps she) went in and led the people, nurturing and taking care of them. After finishing my degrees and absorbing information about the concept of leadership, I'm able to see now that a pastoral role is more involved in leadership than it actually is in "pastorship." The Great Commission that Jesus gave his disciples in Matthew 28 was to go and make disciples.

When I looked at that idea of making disciples, I never really had clarity on that. I always thought that making disciples was going out, maybe evangelizing them, and telling them about Jesus Christ. I never looked at the area of teaching. We see that throughout His ministerial career, if I can call it that, Jesus taught the people. That's mostly what he did. He spent a lot of time teaching them and then He commanded us to teach them.

I don't mind this because all my gifts assessments show that teaching is one of the things God has equipped me to do, but I never really took it seriously until after my DMin. Then I felt equipped and confident to fulfill my mission in life. No longer did I have to ask so many questions or have my thoughts dismissed by someone saying, "That's the way we've always done it." I could think for myself, and think critically, and I found the Bible to be a fresh source of insight and inspiration when I stopped preaching and teaching what I had been told it said and presented it according to what it actually taught.

My research clearly showed that if we don't teach about spiritual gifts, people aren't going to pursue those gifts. If we do teach about them, then people will at least consider them. Then the Holy Spirit can use them to do more because they aren't dismissing their own relevance and importance in God's Kingdom work.

Also, my study confirmed that we as pastors, bishops, elders, or deacons assumed once we became whatever our title was, we were automatically going to be good leaders. It just came with the territory, so to speak, and everything was going to flow smoothly now that we had the title. That of course could not be further from the truth. We thought if we were better theologians, we'd be better leaders, but leadership is a whole separate study and discipline.

At the same time, because we are called to be teachers and disciple-makers, we are constantly teaching, which means we have to have something to give to the people. If we are giving them stale bread and worn-out teachings then the people will become stale and worn out because we are. We just can't be on our same hobby horse, or hammer our same pet doctrines. We have to always be growing ourselves if we want the people to be growing.

I know I could not have chosen a more controversial topic to research: spiritual gifts and their relevance in a Baptist setting. We are dwindling and our people are spiritual malnourished so leadership required that I look at what can be done to better lead the church and my teaching gift wanted to examine what we could the teach that would better lead the church.

As stated earlier, some people in Baptist settings would avoid this topic of gifts and tell me we don't do that—period. My response before my studies was, "Why?" My research changed my question to "why not teach the gifts?" Through my simple experiment, the people grew in biblical knowledge and were more open not just to being a spectator in church to being a participant. After all, isn't Jesus the One building His Church and won't He do that in the power of the Spirit? Then it stands to reason that the Spirit will use the gifts He distributes to the people.

Let me state without hesitancy that the spiritual gifts did not die with the last apostle. They are alive and well today because the Spirit is alive and well, and they should have a greater role in the life of the church. What's more, pastors don't have to have all the gifts. However, pastors do need to lead the church and if they relied more on the gifts in the congregation to teach and equip, they would have more time to lead.

A church could have a pastor equipped with strong administrative gifts, while other people in the church have the stronger vocal gifts—or vice versa. There is nothing that says the pastor must do it all especially if he doesn't have the gift to do it. This is the model we should follow and it's a healthy model. What's more, it's a biblical model. We don't allow anyone to sing in church if they can't sing, but pretty much any other activity is open to people doing things if they don't have the gift. The Church has paid a high price in terms of effectiveness and relevance because we have ignored that truth.

Because we have been content to follow tradition, there is precious little disciple-making going on in our churches. Our pastors ascend the platform, often sit in a big chair, have on special robes, and oversee the service. The people have certain expectations which must be fulfilled every week. Yet there is little teaching going on, and that teaching should be equipping God's people for works of service and ministry.

We have a mandate from Christ that He wants us to disciple His people. The main way we disciple God's people is through teaching. So if we lack disciples, what practice is missing? It is the teaching and it's missing because we have the wrong people teaching or the wrong things being taught. We need to challenge the people to step up and accept their role in the church. They need to challenge us, ask us questions so they can probe our teachings and learn and grow.

We need to change the way we do church and that means none of our traditions are off limits or sacred. The younger generation knows religious tradition; they can sense it a mile away. The Lord said My people perish for the lack of knowledge. There's a direct link between that and the lack of teaching. The Holy Spirit has equipped somebody who's sitting in the congregation to do more than they think they can do, but our teaching and traditions have limited them, as I stated earlier.

Perhaps I will get into this more in my next book, but the church has often tried to "win" with half its team on the bench and by that I mean our women members. They are the lifeblood and support group of any church, especially in the Black Baptist church. We need to do more teaching on women and the role of women in the church to gain better understanding and release them into their purpose.

Maybe my curriculum and teaching can empower, transform, and embolden women to step up and be those leaders for Christ. They are leaders in other organizations or professions, and we are not preventing that. Instead of just saying flat out that women are not to lead or teach, I think we need to examine that, do some research, do some teaching, and allow, as T.D. Jakes would say, the women to be loosed.

It would be my hope that pastors, teachers, and leaders in churches would reevaluate some of their traditional stances where the vocal gifts are concerned and where lay involvement and preaching and teaching are concerned. We have to face the reality of where the church is at.

These are desperate times. We are losing ground constantly to secularism, but the Holy Spirit knows how to build His church. He knows how to equip His people. He knows how to lead and guide us into all the truth. He has gifts that

He bestows on *everyone*. It would seem to me that if we just teach the people, they will know the truth and the truth will set them free.

I know this is going to create more mess. The pastors, rather than doing all the ministry, are going to have to manage and equip and disciple, and the people are going to need to be open to that. And the pastor is going to need to be open to doing it. None of us owns anything in the church—not our ministry, pew, committee place, or role. It's His church and He can do what He wants with it.

Now, I have not included everything in this book from my research, for I knew it was too technical and sometimes got too "deep into the weeds." But if you are interested in this topic and would like to see how your church could grow through some of the teaching I have mentioned, then please contact me. I will make anything I have available to you. Contact me at chaplainDMcGee@gmail.com. Let's pray, talk, and then pioneer something fresh and new for the Lord and His people.

I haven't come this far and done this work not to make a difference. I want to see the church, the black Baptist church, and God's people equipped for success. I want to see the Church grow and I know God wants that too. Where we are is not where we need to be, but I think I have seen with a little faith, mixed with courage, seasoned with biblical teaching, and cooked in good leadership, we can concoct that will be a fragrant aroma to God and a tasty stew for His hungry people. Thank you and God bless you.

APPENDIX

I did not want to make this book a workbook so I did not include all the handouts and materials used during my teaching sessions. I do include some of it here for you to see. If you would like to see more, please contact me and we can discuss structuring sessions for your church. My contact information is at the end of the book.

PRE-CLASS SURVEY

Your Name _____

What is your age?

30-40   40-50   50-60   60-70   70+

What is your gender?

Male   Female

Have you been born again?

Yes   No

How many years have you been part of this church?

_____

1. Do you speak in tongues?

Yes   No

2. Have you ever had the chance to prophecy?

Yes   No

3. Have you ever prayed in the Spirit?

Yes   No

4. Do you believe the Bible lists all the spiritual gifts there are?

Yes   No

5. What spiritual gifts do you believe you have or have expressed in the past?

_____

6. Do you believe that only the pastor is qualified to minister to God's people?

Yes   No

7. If members of the congregation exercised vocal or public spiritual gifts, do you believe that will create confusion and lead to possible error?

Yes   No

8. Are you familiar with Paul's teaching on spiritual gifts?

Yes No

9. Are you open that God may want to use you to express spiritual gifts as a member of His church?

Yes   No

10. Does the thought of exercising a spiritual gift cause you to be afraid?

Yes   No

LESSON ONE

Objectives:

1. Participants will be able to identify the three vocal spiritual gifts and ascertain a broader knowledge of each.
2. Participants will better be able to sense the significance of each vocal gift.
3. Participants will develop a learning posture that will foster individual interest to seek the vocal spiritual gifts.

Introduction

I. The preassessment survey was administered at the beginning of the first session. Time allowed: 30 minutes.

II. Are the vocal spiritual gifts significant? (Class discussion)

III. Why are the vocal spiritual gifts significant?

    A. Jesus states, "new tongues." (Mark 6:17)

    B. We are at war. (Ephesians 6:12)

    C. Christian weapons must be spiritual. (2 Corinthians 10:4)

IV. Significance of tongues, interpretation of tongues, and prophecy?

    A. Personal edification. (1 Corinthians 14:4)

    B. Edification of the church. (1 Corinthians 14:4)

    C. Old Testament overview.

        1. Moses and the children of Israel. (Numbers 11)

        2. Valley of dry bones. (Ezekiel 37:1-14)

        3. Prophetic mandate of God. (Joel 2:28)

LESSON TWO

Objectives

1. At the end of this session, participants will be able to know the difference between tongues and the gift of tongues.
2. Participants interest will be heightened to seek the guidance of the Holy Spirit.
3. Participants will become open to the works of the Holy Spirit.

Tongues and Gift of Tongues

A. Tongues Definition: Oral Roberts defines it as a supernatural utterance by the Holy Spirit.

   1. Not a known intellect.
   2. Acquired through the baptism of the Holy Spirit (Acts 1:8-2:4)
   3. Edifies the whole spirit of man.
   4. Spoken only to God.
   5. Personal prayer language (Jude 20; 1 Corinthians 14:15)

B. Gift of Tongues: Oral Roberts defines this gift as a divine spoken word of God to man to meet a specific need.

   1. Does not come through the baptism of the Holy Spirit.
   2. Differs from personal devotion.
   3. Spoken through the spiritual being of man.
   4. Morton Kelsey relates it to the psychology of C. G. Jung.

C. Biblical use of tongues

   1. Gift of tongues must be interpreted. (1 Corinthians 14:13)
   2. Interpretation must always follow. (1 Corinthians 14:27-28)

3. Fear of interpretation must be removed. (Oral Roberts: Open your mouth and began to speak)
4. Are imparted to meet the needs of others. (Oral Roberts)

LESSON THREE

Objectives:

1. At the end of this session, participants will have knowledge regarding the interpretation of tongues.
2. Participants may sense the urgency to seek and possibly interpret a divine word.
3. Participants will choose to become sensitive to the voice of God.

Interpretation of Tongues

I. Interpretation of Tongues

Definition

1. A word spoken by God to man to meet the needs of others (edification comes through interpretation.)
2. Interpretation is not a translation.
3. Interpretation is the same as prophecy.
4. Spoken through the spiritual being of man

II. Interpretation communicates intelligently what was uttered by the Spirit

    A. May trigger other gifts. (Acts 19:6)

    B. The difference between interpretation and prophecy.

    C. Relationship between interpretation and prophecy.

III. Pray to interpret.

    A. Interpretation is given to the one speaking.

    B. The speaker must pray to interpret.

    C. Uninterpreted tongues are forbidden in the public (1 Corinthians 14:28.)

    D. Tongues and Interpretation of tongues can be given to bring healing and encouragement to overcome distress and disease.

LESSON FOUR

Objectives:

1. Participants will gain general knowledge of the gift of prophecy and its purpose.
2. Participants will sense the voice of God and become confident to prophesy.
3. Participants will become willing to submit to the works of the Holy Spirit and affirm the gift of prophecy.

Prophecy

A. Prophecy definition

    1. Supernatural utterance in a known tongue

    2. Word spoken directly from God to man

    3. Spoken in a known intellect

B. Purpose (1 Corinthians 14:3)

    1. Edification to the body of believers

    2. Exhortation – motivate the church

    3. Consolation – comfort in times of tribulation

C. Characteristics of prophecy

    1. Superior gift (1 Corinthians 14:31)

    2. Gift for all (1 Corinthians 14:31)

    3. Indication of God's approval

    4. Must be done "decently and in order"

    5. Must be subject to being judged (1 Corinthians 14:29)

    6. Must be in alignment with the word of God

LESSON FIVE

Objectives:

1. At the end of this session, participants will understand that vocal spiritual gifts are for the modern-day church.
2. Participants will better be able to assess their personal relationship with Christ.
3. Participants will seek the Holy Spirit to be baptized with the Holy Spirit.

Modern Day Use of the Vocal Spiritual Gifts

I. Are vocal spiritual gifts for today?

    A. Stumbling blocks to modern day usage.

        1. Secularization – watering away from the word of God.

        2. Watering down the word of God.

        3. Cessationism – gifts ended in Bible days.

        4. Hierarchy – Church doctrine and government dismiss the works of the Holy Spirit

II. Reestablish relationship with God – seek a closer walk

    A. Embrace the possibility of gifts today.

        1. God's church must operate through works of the Holy Spirit.

        2. Gifts are to be expressed for the common good.

    B. Reclaim your God given character.

        1. Be gifted and nurtured by God's Spirit.

        2. Become empowered for service (Acts 1:8)

        3. Difference between cessationist and Pentecostals

   4. Be filled with the Spirit
  C. Seek the baptism of the Holy Spirit
   1. Ask
   2. Believe
   3. Receive
III. Modern-day encounters—Jack Deere analogy of learning the language.

LESSON SIX

There is no more controversial or divisive topic in churches than the practice of speaking or praying in tongues. Here is the material I drew from when I taught the people in my church who attended my sessions.

Tongues and the Gift of Tongues

Section 1

Oral Roberts defined tongues as a supernatural utterance given by the Holy Spirit. Roberts further noted that tongues is not a known dialect. It is unknown to the speaker but understood by the Holy Spirit. It is the Spirit of man communing with God. Tongues are acquired through the baptism of the Holy Spirit (see Acts 1:8-2:4). This experience is subsequent to conversion. Roberts identifies this experience as personal prayer language or private devotion to God (see Jude 20; 1 Corinthians 14:15).

Tongues edifies the whole spirit of man. This private devotion is spoken only to God. Paul stated,

> And in the same way the Spirit also helps our weakness; for we do not know how to pray as we should, but the Spirit Himself intercedes for us with groaning too deep for words; and He who searches the hearts knows what the mind of the Spirit is, because He intercedes for the saints according to the will of God (Romans 8:26-27).

The Gift of Tongues

In this experience God speaks through the spirit of man. A divine connection exists between God and the designated person to whom God chooses to release this gift in a public setting so the unbeliever will see the manifestation of God and surrender their life to Christ. This gift does not come from the baptism of the Holy Spirit.

Morton T. Kelsey states in *Tongue Speaking*, "Tongues is a leaven that works in your life to bring about God's end, because it takes a man that has left the church and returns him back to the priesthood, and it transforms a man that has attended church for years through habit and brings him into a personal relationship with Jesus Christ."[115] Kelsey emphasizes a difference of reaction regarding the tongues phenomenon in the local church has continued. It is noted that many Christian churches have chosen to affirm and practice this biblically-based phenomenon, while older churches look through the scope of suspicion and hold that such practices have no place in the modern church. Kelsey further notes the conclusion of this train of thought by stating,

> It is merely emotional indulgence in sheer irrationality in the name of religion, a return to a more primitive kind of religion. As these people see it, this practice has no place in the highly developed ethical religion of today.[116]

Despite this viewpoint held in the older churches, Kelsey has observed significant church growth in the Pentecostal churches that stress speaking in tongues. Kelsey writes insightfully in his section titled "Controversy in the Established Churches,"

> While the more conventional, established churches have barely kept pace with the population explosion in the United States, these fundamentalistic and enthusiastic groups have skyrocketed in membership to seventh place, and have sprung up in every city throughout the country.[117]

Pentecostals appear to adhere strictly to the biblical evidence that tongues are the initial evidence of Spirit baptism, and they further hold that this experience is to be experienced today. Kelsey concurs, writing, "Glossolalia is the evidence, indeed, that one has been given a new spiritual endowment, the gift of the Holy Spirit."[118] This experience has

---
[115] Morton T. Kelsey, *Tongue Speaking* (Garden City, NY: Doubleday & Company, 1964), 4.
[116] Kelsey, 4.
[117] Kelsey, 5.
[118] Kelsey, 6.

been evident not only in the Pentecostal church but has spread abroad to others, such as Baptist, Lutheran, Presbyterian, and Episcopalian churches.

Kelsey further alludes to the fact that this tongues phenomenon has drawn the interest of depth psychology (which describes approaches to therapy and research that take the unconscious into account). Based upon this possibility, Kelsey maintained it would be unwise to dismiss this phenomenon of tongues and depth Pentecostal religion as meaningless. Kelsey describes the psychology of C. G. Jung relating to these phenomena of tongues by stating,

> Jung came to the conclusion that there are levels of the unconscious beyond the personal, the buried memories, and the primitive impulses of the id. He believed that man is in touch with an objective realm of psychic reality containing elements both inferior and superior to human consciousness.[119]

Jung's conclusion has resulted from empirical evidence of thousands of patients over a fifty-year period. Kelsey concludes by stating, "Jung found speaking in tongues is one evidence of a breakthrough of this objective psyche or deep, collective level of the unconscious."[120]

As we will examine in the next lesson, the gift of tongues must always be interpreted. (1 Corinthians 14:13; 27-28) People may experience the world of fear and choose not to speak the interpretation. Roberts explains that after the speaker prays for the interpretation, they must open their mouth and begin to speak what the Holy Spirit give them. It may not be a complete sentence, but it will be the divine word of God to meet a specific need. Roberts further explained that the specific need could be a person may be facing a certain situation. Then God will give a divine word that will be a specific answer for that individual in such a way that they know it was God who has spoken because only He knew their situational need.

---

[119]Kelsey, 7.
[120]Kelsey, 9.

LESSON SEVEN

INTERPRETATION OF TONGUES

The interpretation of tongues is a word spoken by God in a known dialect to edify or meet the needs of others. Interpretation is not a translation. Siegfried Schatzmann stressed the significance of interpretation in that "what makes interpretation of tongues indispensable is its function of communicating intelligibly and intelligently, with the mind, what was uttered in the Spirit, by the glossolalist."[121]

Schatzmann, when examining Paul's thinking on this subject, observed that the gift of tongues and the interpretation of tongues are restricted in usage. He further pointed out that the Pauline narrative links these two gifts: "It is the interpretation of tongues which edifies; therefore, at least in terms of effect, it becomes a gift equivalent to prophecy."[122] There is a distinct difference between the gift of prophecy and the interpretation of tongues, but they are linked together, for they serve the same function, which is to edify.

Paul clearly stated, "Now I wish that you all spoke in tongues, but even more that you would prophesy; and greater is one who prophesies than one who speaks in tongues, unless he interprets, so that the church may receive edifying" (1 Corinthians 14:5). Schatzmann clarified this distinction by stating, "The former is God's revelation addressed to persons in their need, whereas the latter is the intelligible communication of glossolalic utterance addressed to God."[123] However, interpretation is not the same translation.

Schatzmann further clarified that the noun (interpretation) is not the same as "translation" as in the case of foreign languages but rather the translation serves as an explanation. Schatzmann further concludes, "Anthony Thiselton has advanced the alternate meaning of 'to put into words' for interpretation. But there may not be as much new ground broken

---

[121]Siegfried S. Schatzmann, *A Pauline Theology of Charismata* (Peabody, MA: Hendrickson, 1987), 43.

[122]Schatzmann, 43.

[123]Schatzmann, 43.

as Thiselton proposes, for 'to put into words' and 'to explain' are but different expressions of the same notion."[124]

My own research on this topic showed a strong link between the concept of the interpretation of tongues and a prophetic word from the Lord. Mark Cartledge states in *Charismatic Glossolalia*, "Pentecostals believe that, with the gift of interpretation of tongues, the church congregation might edified. Speaking in tongues edifies the speaker, but in the public the person must keep quiet unless someone is able to interpret the tongue."[125] Therefore, both glossolalia and prophecy have parallel functions when the former is interpreted. This is believed to be the reason that Paul stressed the significance of interpretation.

Arnold Bittlinger wrote, "Interpretation is a complementary gift which makes possible and meaningful the use of tongues in the meeting for worship."[126] He noted that the gift of tongues takes on real meaning in the church. The individual praying to God in the Spirit likewise receives the interpretation from God. However, it is through this type of prayer that the church receives edification. Bittlinger further added, "Paul ranks 'prayer in the Spirit,' when interpreted, as equal in value in building up the church, to prophecy the most desirable gift (1 Corinthians 14:5)"[127]

As with other scholars in my research, Bittlinger affirmed that the gift of interpretation is given to the one praying in the Spirit or to another person, but either way, the interpretation is just as important as the gift of tongues:

> The gift of tongues when interpreted is equal in value to prophecy in the building up of the church; 'He who prophesies is greater than he who speaks in tongues, unless someone interprets, so that the church may be edified' (1 Corinthians 14:5).

---

[124] Schatzmann, 43.

[125] Mark J. Cartledge, *Charismatic Glossolalia: An Empirical Theological Study* (Burlington, VT: Ashgate, 2002), 78.

[126] Arnold Bittlinger, Gifts and Grace, A Commentary on I Corinthians 12-14 (Grand Rapids, MI: Eerdmans, 1968), 51.

[127] Bittlinger, 52.

'Therefore, he who speaks in a tongue should pray for the power to interpret" '(1 Corinthians 14:13).[128]

Additionally, it is noted that Paul evaluated the effectiveness or propriety of the gift of tongues when it was used in a public environment. Uninterpreted tongues were forbidden in the public setting, whereas its use in private devotion was encouraged. Bittlinger compared this gift of tongues with a foreign language. If one speaks in a foreign language to a group that does not understand the language, one would need to translate. Therefore, it is seen that the foreign language and the gift of tongues need to be translated and interpreted so others can comprehend. Bittlinger concluded with what Paul wrote: "In church I would rather speak five words with my mind, in order to instruct others, than ten thousand words in a tongue" (14:19).[129]

Finally, Dr. Paul King, in *God's Healing Arsenal*, insightfully added, "Sometimes God gives words of prophecy, supernatural knowledge or wisdom, tongues and interpretation, discernment of spirits, special mountain-moving faith in order to bring healing and encouragement and direction to overcome your distress and disease"[130] and "sometimes through interpretation of tongues or a resulting word of wisdom or knowledge the Holy Spirit gives a word in due season, a timely word of counsel or insight for the situation."[131]

---

[128] Bittlinger, 101.

[129] Bittlinger, 104.

[130] Paul L. King, God's Healing Arsenal (Alachua, FL: Bridge Logos Foundation, 2011), 109.

[131] King, 281.

LESSON EIGHT

PROPHECY

In a session of "The Holy Spirit in the Now" lectures, Oral Roberts addressed the gift of prophecy and stated, "Prophecy is an inspired utterance by a human being or believer, inspired by the Holy Spirit."[132] The manifestation of this gift is to edify, exhort, and profit. Prophecy is composed of words chosen by the Holy Spirit, not by man's own intellect. Roberts noted that God speaks to man in many different ways. One of the ways is through the Word of God. Roberts clearly pointed out that prophecy is an inspired utterance and may come in the form of a verse in the Bible.[133]

C. Peter Wagner defined prophecy as "The special ability that God gives to certain members of the Body of Christ to receive and communicate an immediate message of God to His people through a divinely anointed utterance."[134] Some may find problems with the gift of prophecy in that they do not feel all people can hear from God. However, Wagner wrote, "In some cases, it might be our own fault because we do not try hard enough or because we are not filled with the Holy Spirit or because there is some sin in our lives blocking our relationship with God."[135]

Wayne Grudem commented, "The main function of Old Testament prophets was to be messengers from God, sent to speak to men and women with words of God."[136] The words of the Old Testament prophet were divinely given by God. However, he added, "The New Testament prophet/apostle was commissioned by Christ and sent to do a specific mission for Him"[137] Prophecy is a sign to the believer. The inspired words

---

[132]Oral Roberts. 'The Gift of Prophecy," n.p., The Holy Spirit in the Now on CDROM, ORU HSC#5. spring 1974.

[133]Roberts, 'The Gift of Prophecy," CD-ROM.

[134]C. Peter Wagner, *Apostles and Prophets: The Foundation of the Church* (Ventura, CA: Regal, 2000), 96.

[135]Wagner, 97.

[136]Grudem, *The Gift of Prophecy* (Eastbourne, UK: Kingsway, 1988), 17.

[137]Grudem, *The Gift of Prophecy*, 25.

of the prophet are given to bless others. Grudem pointed out, "Prophecy is an indication of God's approval and blessing on the congregation because it shows that God is actively present in the assembled church."[138]

Prophecies prove to make an impact in the life of the outsider. Grudem insightfully writes,

> "If an outsider comes in and everyone prophesies, one will be speaking about the secrets of the outsider's hear, which he thought no one knew. He will realize these prophesies must be the result of God's working, and he will fall on his face and declare, 'Truly God is among you.'"[139]

In *The Gift of Prophecy*, John Wimber stated, "The gift of prophecy is generally a message of strengthening, encouragement, and comfort. It's an inspired message for the moment in the common language and could be prefaced by 'Now hear this.'"[140] Prophecy may have a negative influence on some Christians because it involves subjective experience. People have less of a problem accepting preaching, teaching, and even Bible study as ways God speaks to Christians because of their familiarity of it being rooted in Scripture.

While all Christians agree that Scripture is authoritative and authentic revelation of God, not all interpret it the same. Wimber observed, "Some Christians even maintain that belief in more subjective expressions of God's communication opens the door to emotional delusion or, worse yet, satanic deception. Their position is not that God could not speak today in these ways, but He has chosen not to."[141]

However, there are ways to prevent the pitfalls of subjective revelation and to authenticate the message of the prophet. Wimber turned to Scripture to ensure that Christians are not

---

[138] Wayne Grudem, "1 Corinthians 14:20-25: Prophecy and Tongues as a Sign of God's Attitude," Westminster Theological Journal 41 (1979): 391.

[139] Grudem, "l Corinthians 14:20-25: Prophecy and Tongues as a Sign of God's Attitude," 392.

[140] John Wimber, 'The Gift of Prophecy," Charisma November (1992): 53.

[141] Wimber, 54.

led astray by prophetic words. Wimber used a seven-points guideline to provide assurance that Scripture will ensure Christians are not led astray by prophetic words:

> Personal prophecy should glorify the Word of God, Jesus Christ. Prophetic messages should conform to the Word of God, the Bible. Prophecy should not be used to establish doctrine or practice. Those who deliver a prophetic word should be of sound moral character, submitted to the lordship of Jesus and producing good fruit in their ministry. Prophetic messages should be given in the Spirit of love (l Corinthians 14:3; James 3:17). No one should make major decisions based on personal prophetic words alone (1 Corinthians 14:27-32). Many, if not most, personal prophetic words given today are conditional and, as such, are invitations not certainties (Jeremiah 18:7-10)"[142]

Paul identified prophecy as the superior gift for a specific reason.

> Pursue love, yet desire earnestly spiritual gifts, but especially that you may prophesy. For one who in a tongue does not speak to men, but to God; for no one understands but, in his spirit, he speaks mysteries. But one who prophesies speaks to men for edification and exhortation and consolation. One who speaks in a tongue edifies himself; but one who prophesies edifies the church (1 Corinthians 14:1-4).

Paul further notes that all can prophesy. Bruce Yocum wrote,

> It is evident that in the life of the early Church the communities expected that the Spirit would manifest Himself in ministries and services which might fall within the spectrum which extends from A to P, but they also expected the Spirit to manifest

---
[142]Wimber, 54-55.

himself in the other ministries and services within the section of the spectrum which extends from P to Z.[143]

Lack of awareness and fear are believed to be the main contributors to decreased prophetic activity in the Church today. Yocum suggested,

> Even where the diminishing of this gift has been seen in the Church and some believe that only certain people have this gift, God is taking care of the first problem, in that Christians today are experiencing the real possibility of receiving prophecy.[144]

The fear of abuse and misuse of the prophetic gift has to be overcome by the individual. Yocum concluded, "Fear is evidence of a lack of faith in God."[145] Prophecy must submit to being tested. Paul states, "And let two or three prophets speak, and let the others pass judgment" (1 Corinthians 14:29). Paul was clear in that when prophets speak, it is to be done decently and in order, and the prophets are subject to being judged for authenticity and accuracy by others.

---

[143]Yocum, 134.
[144]Yocum, 135.
[145]Yocum 138.

LESSON NINE

Let me pause before we move on and summarize for you. There is an abundance of material from respected authors and commentators that should give us cause to re-evaluate our approach to the Spirit and the gifts. This is what I attempted to impart to my church during my DMin project—that the Spirit was alive and well, and wanted to use them, not just the pastor, in the work and life of the church. The Apostle Paul taught about the gifts, including the vocal gifts, and used them to teach about the nature of the church or ecclesiology, which is simply a sophisticated word for the theology of the church—what it is, why it exists, and what God wants to do with it through Christ.

So now I have established that there is at least no small amount of spiritual evidence for spiritual gifts and their relevance for the church and believers. I hope you will consider your own stance toward this important issue. As you do, let's move on in the next chapter to my DMin project itself and give you some of the particulars of what I did and how I did it. I will not be able to share all that was involved, but at the end of the book, I tell you how to get in touch with me, for I would be only too glad to share more about my experience and the specific resources I developed for my project.

MODERN USE OF THE VOCAL SPIRITUAL GIFTS

Bruce Yocum noted,

> The world around the Christian community is changing, and powerful forces are at work which opposes the proclamation of the Gospel. The only response is a Christianity which visibly demonstrates and relies upon the power of God, a Church which fulfills its prophetic role. The operation of the prophetic gifts is only one aspect of the renewal in spiritual power which we so desperately need, but it is an important aspect. In the first century, God spoke through the prophets to the Christian

Churches, giving them warning, guidance and direction. Today, God desires to speak directly and clearly to the Christian Churches, warning them, building them. and giving them direction.[146]

Is there a need for prophecy in our churches today? Paul valued this gift highly and told the Corinthian church to make love their aim but to earnestly desire the gift of prophecy: "Pursue love, yet desire earnestly spiritual gifts, but especially that you may prophecy" (1 Corinthians 14:1). Grudem commented that "If Paul was eager for the gift of prophecy to function at Corinth, troubled as the church was by immaturity selfishness, divisions and other problems, then should we not also be eager for this gift to function once again in our churches today?"[147]

Grudem further believed that if the churches followed the taught word regarding prophecy, the church would receive benefits:

> First, neglecting prophecy in the church is being disobedient to scripture, and this is reason enough to believe that the church will have negative consequences eternally and will lack in receiving their full blessing if they obeyed. Second, if this gift is allowed to function and is encouraged in our lives, it would add an element of closeness to God and sensitivity to His promptings in our daily walk.[148]

Therefore, benefits could even extend to making worship services richer and cause people to be in awe as they beheld the manifest presence of God. The church would be better edified through the presence of God and the divine revelation given from that presence.

Gary Charles provided a modern-day perspective of spiritual gifts in the local church. Charles affirmed that the diversity of gifts in the Corinthian church resulted in disunity,

---

[146] Grudem, The Gift of Prophecy, 265.

[147] Grudem, The Gift of Prophecy, 266.

[148] Gary Charles, "1 Corinthians 12:1-13." Charisma: Peer Review. Interpretation 44, no. 1 (1990), 66.

and he suggested this problem stemmed from a life centered around false hierarchy. This is why Paul was so persistent in his argument that all spiritual gifts come from God and are to bear witness of Jesus Christ. Charles wrote, "This text's emphasis on gifts given for the common good warrants a fresh reading by the modern church."[149]

Today when the sociological and cultural climate fosters individualism, the church is placed in a vulnerable state. I believe the church can have a new experience if members chose to embrace the diversity of gifts. Charles is of the opinion that this practice could foster church growth as opposed to utilizing gimmicks disguised as evangelism. He concluded with the importance of this text:

> In 1 Corinthians 12:1-13 Paul states his understanding of a genuinely charismatic church. First, a charismatic church recognizes that the gifts of God's Spirit are given to every Christian, not just to a fortunate few. Secondly, charismatic Christianity accepts spiritual gifts for practical use and ministry, not simply for display. Finally, the truly charismatic church knows that Christian unity is not a personal achievement but a remarkable gift from God. To treat this text seriously invites the church to reclaim its God-given character. Gifted and nurtured by God's Spirit, the church exists neither to enable Christians to reach the heights of ecstatic spiritual experience nor simply to bless the piety. The church exists to glorify Jesus as its Lord, to live by God's life-giving Spirit, and to invite all Christians to express their gifts in the way in which they were intended—for the common good."[150]

It is time that churches reclaim their God-given character. Luke wrote, "And He called the twelve together, and gave them power and authority over all the demons, and to heal diseases. And He sent them out to proclaim the kingdom of

---

[149]Charles, 67.
[150]Charles, 68.

God, and to perform healings" (Luke 9:1, 2). The power and authority of Jesus Christ has made the churches proclaimers and workers. Neither an individual's power nor their status that allows them to be proclaimers, but it is the mighty powerful name of Jesus Christ.

Christ desires that believers become empowered and filled with the Holy Spirit. This empowerment is the catalyst to the church becoming vibrant and not stagnant. God does not want the church to be quenchers of the Holy Spirit, but proclaimers on the truth under the Spirit's anointing and leading.

Paul exhorted the church to be filled with the Spirit. Luke recorded that Jesus promises the church would receive power after that the Holy Spirit had come upon them (see Acts 1:8). I understand that on the Day of Pentecost the Holy Spirit empowered the church as they were all filled with the Holy Spirit and began to give the outward sign of speaking with other tongues.

The modern church may do well to defragment their mental hard drive and seek God and the person of the Holy Spirit. Paul was clear when he stated, "Therefore if any man is in Christ, he is a new creature; the old things passed away; behold, new things have come" (2 Corinthians 5:17). The modern church needs to put away the old way of thinking and see that Christ is alive and well and wants the church to walk in the newness of Christ. Churches need to marry the idea that God has not stopped doing miracles.

Churches cannot afford to remain cessationist while they lack growth. Maybe the Pentecostals, charismatics, and other full gospel movements possess a treasure that would be valuable to all churches. The Bible is clear that "you have not because you ask not" (James 4:2). We need to ask the Holy Spirit to fill our souls. Individuals have to believe and be in expectation of that infilling.

Then we shall receive the baptism of the Holy Spirit. Remember the utterance will not be in our known language. This is not the natural man at work in our lives; it is the work of the Holy Spirit. There has to be a shift from the physical man to the Spirit of God. God is a mysterious God. God said, "For my thoughts are not your thoughts, neither are your ways My ways, declares the Lord" (Isaiah 55:8).

In *Surprised by the Voice of God,"* Jack Deere offered great insight into learning the language of the Holy Spirit when he, a former Baptist, came into the knowledge of how God communicates with people today. Deere stated in his narrative titled "Learning the Language of the Holy Spirit" that

> I had been trained to teach the Bible, but I didn't have a clue about bringing a revelation, a tongue, or an interpretation. Nor did I understand how the other supernatural gifts functioned, gifts like words of wisdom, words of knowledge, the gift of faith, the gift of healing or miracles, or the gift of distinguishing spirits and so on (1 Corinthians 12:8-10).[151]

The only part of the Holy Spirit language he understood was the written word of God. This caused Deere to wonder how much of his understanding was created through the years of traditional teaching and how much was really illuminated through the work of the Holy Spirit. During the primitive stage of Deere learning the language, he found three positive areas in his life.

> First, I had an acute sense of his spiritual poverty, second, I had come to believe God was still speaking in all the ways that He spoke in the Bible, and third, I knew I needed God to speak to me in more personal ways if I was ever going to experience the kind of church life described in the New Testament.[152]

Deere offered a significant analogy to learning the language of the Holy Spirit. In his analogy, Deere talked about how he had studied German for several years, but later went to live in a small village in Germany. It was in this small

---

[151] Jack Deere, *Surprised by the Voice of God* (Grand Rapids, MI: Zondervan, 1996), 167.
[152] Deere, 168.

German village that Deere found himself surrounded by people speaking the dialect, and it was not very long before Deere became fluent in the dialect. Therefore, Deere concluded the best way to learn the language of the Holy Spirit is to be in the environment of those that speak the language. This environment allows people to progress more rapidly than in those who do not speak in the dialect.

CONCLUSION

There you have my general overview of my research that caused me to conclude that the vocal spiritual gifts are relevant for and to be deployed in modern local churches. I attempted also to give you an idea of what I taught the members of my congregation who participated in my D/Min. research project. The results were as I expected. After I taught about the vocal gifts, people were more open to expressing them and gained confidence that they had something to do to help the church grow, besides simply attending public services.

My purpose in writing was not to give you a total download of my workshops or my research. My intent was to challenge you to consider what else you can do to release the power that is sitting in our church pews every Sunday. What can you do to equip our people to accept and then release the gifts that Paul said the Spirit has given to every believer? If you are not a leader, what can you do to be more adept at the use of your spiritual gifts? The Church of Jesus Christ finds itself in a crisis, but God knows how to get us out of it, but it will require all of us, leaders and followers, to do our part to see that the power no longer stays dormant, but is released for the good of the saints and the glory of God.

TO CONTACT DWIGHT MCGEE, EMAIL HIM AT:

CHAPLAINDMCGEE@GMAIL.COM

www.ingramcontent.com/pod-product-compliance
Lightning Source LLC
LaVergne TN
LVHW051506070426
835507LV00022B/2954